SOARING FOR THE KINGDOM

Delsa Christian

© Copyright 2022 by Delsa Christian

First Edition

ISBN-13: 979-8-9851043-1-8

Written and Published by KingdomEncounter

Edited by: Becky Blanton

All rights reserved. No part of this publication may be reproduced, stored in or
introduced into a retrieval system, or transmitted in any form or by any means
(electronic, mechanical, photocopying, recording, or otherwise) without the prior
written permission of both the copyright holder and above publisher of this book. Please
do not participate in or encourage electronic piracy of copyrighted materials. To get
permission to quote portions of this book, order bulk copies, or other questions, please
contact:

delsachristian@kingdomencounter19.com

God has anointed you to **soar**. So, soar.

" I can do all things through Him who strengthens me."

— *Philippians 4:13 ESV*

"But those who hope in the Lord will renew their strength.
They will soar on wings like eagles; they will run and not
grow weary; they will walk and not be faint."

— *Isaiah 40:31 NLT*

"Do not be conformed to this world, but be transformed by
the renewal of your mind, that by testing you may discern
what is the will of God, what is good and acceptable and
perfect."

— *Romans 12:2*

Contents

Introduction — The Four-Part Foundation and Six Aspects You Need to SOAR	vii
1. Spiritual Nourishment	1
2. Organize Your Life	15
3. Accountable To God And Man	38
4. Release Yourself from all Encumbrances	47
5. The Six Aspects of Living: An Overview of the Basic Structure of All Human Beings	62
6. Aspect Number One: Seek an Emotional Balance	80
7. Aspect Number Two: Seek A Physical Balance	99
8. Aspect Number Three: Seek a Spiritual Balance	110
9. Aspect Number Four: Seek a Social Balance	117
10. Aspect Number Five — Seek a Psychological Balance	129
11. Aspect Number Six — Seek a Purpose Balance	138
12. SOARing High for the Kingdom	145
Before You Go	161
Acknowledgments	163
About the Author	165
Notes	167

Introduction – The Four-Part Foundation and Six Aspects You Need to SOAR

This book is about laying the foundation to SOAR and building the six life skills that we need to live the bountiful, fruitful life God promised us.

THE SOAR FOUNDATION AND ASPECTS

Nothing stands without a foundation. Buildings don't, societies don't nor religions, beliefs, or people. Foundations are so important, that the Bible mentions them more than 40 times! And one of my favorite scriptures about foundations is:

> *"For no one can lay a foundation other than that which is laid, which is Jesus Christ."*
>
> — *I Corinthians 3:11.*

When you learn how to create a healthy foundation built upon a personal relationship with Jesus Christ, everything you build will stand and flourish throughout your life with love and truth

Introduction – The Four-Part Foundation and Six Aspects You Need to...

abounding. The real question to ask then is, "How can I attain this life?"

The ANSWER?

Through extensive research and years of practice, I've taken the time to develop a powerful process that I will share with you throughout this book that will allow you to not only develop, but more importantly, sustain the life-changing foundation to walk with Jesus daily. I will take you by the hand and guide you, step by step, on a life-long path building upon the following four biblical foundational elements I call SOAR to achieve this walk with God:

SOAR is an acronym that stands for:

S — Seeking spiritual nourishment.

O — Organizing your life, to pursue an ordered path.

A — Accounting to God.

R — Releasing all of your encumbrances.

Next, building from these four foundations, I will share what I call "The Six Pillars of Living." These are essential life skills that you will learn to enable you to achieve a healthy, daily, Kingdom-focused life. They are as follows:

1. **Emotional** – Your emotional life is centered more around your heart than your mind. It's about understanding that we all have emotions that are both good and, at time, not so good. Here, your focus should be on managing your emotions so that they serve you, other, and, most of all God. I will share with you ways you can better manage your emotions to help support your growth and success in work and life.

viii

Introduction — The Four-Part Foundation and Six Aspects You Need to...

2. **Physical** - We are responsible for our good health which looks like regular self care of our mind and body. This chapter offers a cornucopia of wisdom I've learned and tested again and again to help you develop a very healthy God-centered daily living experience.

3. **Spiritual** - Contrast "spiritual" with not just believing in God but building and sustaining a personal relationship with him through prayer and gratitude. Here, you will learn even more how to build a spiritual life in your everyday world.

4. **Social** – These skills are part of both your business and personal network. Here, questions for to answer include whether you are surrounded by the right people—those who have similar and complementary values to yours. These are people who believe in living a God-centered life. They are people who committed to the SOAR foundation. There are some people we shouldn't be around. This skill is about prioritizing your inner circle. Jesus had the 12, then the 3. Give and take or better yet, *exchange* support regularly with other like-valued people.I'll show you how to discover and invite those special partners who can help you and you them build a life with God at the center.

5. **Psychological** – This is a focus on mindsets. It's about building a leadership mindset. Paradoxically when you build a strong *leadership* mindset you benefit even more by becoming a follower of God, building a daily disciplined, spiritual path. Here, you then find yourself at the doorstep of a significant relationship with God.

6. **Purpose** – Finally, there is the very important skill of determining your purpose and then living it daily. So many people struggle with first, discovering their purpose and then leading with it. Your purpose can and very well may change throughout your life, but I have found that those who reach for and tap into the purpose thread inside of

Introduction — The Four-Part Foundation and Six Aspects You Need to...

them that connects to God's will for them, are those who truly live rich lives. In this chapter I'll take your hand and show you how to connect your purpose with God's will.

If you start to see any of The Six Pillars start slipping in your life, don't worry. You can return to the SOAR foundation and rebuild again. Note that while SOARING for the Kingdom is a lifelong learning process, don't be discouraged if you slip. If you stay with me and stay committed (and again, I'm here to hold your hand through the words I share in this book) you will see amazing results in 90 days. And to help you even more, I've created a special *90-day* journal for you to help you.

> NOTE: There is great significance in the number 90. In the business world, for example, businesses run on quarterly reviews, which, of course, are 90 days.
>
> Also, 90 days is typically the trial period for new employees. In our private lives, consider the significance of the first trimester of a gestating baby. Additionally, 90 days is what experts have come to know as the real-time it takes to master something. Many people are under the false assumption that 30 days is the timing. Yes, that might be the timing to form a habit but to master the habit takes an additional 60 days. The ultimate goal during the development of any skill or process though is really about partnering with God to establish a focus and a goal for any endeavor. So just relax and enjoy the journey. You are in the perfect hands of God.

None of us is perfect. Perfection fled mankind the instant Adam and Eve disobeyed God. We've all been struggling with decay and imperfection since then. This doesn't mean God can't or hasn't given us new hearts. We *can* live better, cope with chaos and crisis, and utilize a variety of methods to remediate life's many issues. Through

Introduction — The Four-Part Foundation and Six Aspects You Need to...

the life skills I'll share with you throughout this book, you can lighten our load, avoid drama, and find a better, more blessed life.

Finding your passion, pursuing your purpose, and enjoying your life are difficult accomplishments for anyone, believers or not. If we didn't grow up in a healthy, nurturing, and supporting family who served God — as so many of us didn't — it can be even more challenging. I was one of the fortunate ones who met and embraced God early and, as a result, learned a number of basic life skills at a young age. Having grown up with a strong spiritual, emotional, and mental foundation, I now passionately want to help you learn the things I have found to be so rewarding — which means building healthy thoughts and emotions and creating a solid spiritual foundation built on reading, praying, studying, and knowing the Word of God.

Life, when lived in the will of God and following the kind of life He created for us to live, is amazing. We have a purpose, peace, and fellowship with our Creator and fellow human beings in a way I can't describe. It must be experienced. Further, I know that this book will help you realize how to pursue a life that allows you to SOAR for and in the Kingdom of God. I pray for a life for you where you find your purpose in God and begin to SOAR with that purpose.

From His command to the priests to build all altars with four corners and four pillars to the New Jerusalem having four walls, we see how critical the number **four** is to God. The system I've laid out for you to follow is based on this four-part foundation centered and focused on principles God sets out in the Bible:

> *"THEREFORE THEN, since we are surrounded by so great a*
> *cloud of witnesses [who have borne testimony to the*
> *Truth], let us strip off and throw aside every encumbrance*
> *(unnecessary weight) and that sin which so readily (deftly*
> *and cleverly) clings to and entangles us, and let us run*
> *with patient endurance and steady and active persistence,*

Introduction — The Four-Part Foundation and Six Aspects You Need to...

> *the appointed course of the race that is set before us,*
> *Looking away [from all that will distract] to Jesus, Who is*
> *the Leader and the Source of our faith [giving the first*
> *incentive for our belief] and is also its Finisher [bringing*
> *it to maturity and perfection]. He, for the joy [of obtaining*
> *the prize] that was set before Him, endured the cross,*
> *despising and ignoring the shame, and is now seated at the*
> *right hand of the throne of God."*
>
> *— Hebrews 12:1-2*

"Throw aside every encumbrance" so you can SOAR. Release Yourself from all Encumbrances through Christ from bondage, sin, and anything that separates you from God and prevents you from soaring is critical. We cannot reach the pinnacle if we are carrying weight. Release bad habits, hurts, unforgiveness, anger, and regrets, so you let go of the things holding you down. Get rid of the "cage" built from these hindrances.

By following the biblical foundations I have illuminated here and trusting in the triune of God, Jesus Christ, and the Holy Spirit to do the work in us, I know you will be transformed just as Christ promised. We get a new heart and are transformed mentally, emotionally, spiritually, and physically. Are you ready? Let's begin!

> *"Therefore, if anyone is in Christ, he is a new creation; old*
> *things have passed away; behold, all things have become*
> *new." Once you are in Christ, you go through a spiritual*
> *transformation; your old self is gone, you are new!"*
>
> *— 2 Corinthians 5:17*

Chapter 1

Spiritual Nourishment

S — *Seek spiritual nourishment.*

Everything Rob needed to know to get the sports car in front of him running again, was in "The Books." Rob, 13, wanted a sports car for his 16th birthday. He was crazy about them. His room had posters and photos and models of sports cars. He wore t-shirts with cars on them. A sports car was, he told his father, the one thing he wanted most in the world and he was willing to do anything to get it.

His parents could afford to buy him a car, but they wanted more for him. So, they found an old, once very expensive, convertible sports car. A mechanic assured them it would run again if it had a lot of work done on it. Labor, he told them, would be the largest cost, but the parts would be affordable. So, they bought it and had it towed home, a gift for Rob's 14th birthday. They also bought all the shop manuals and how-to books and basic tools for him to use to work on the car.

"The car is yours, and we'll pay half the insurance on it until you're 21, if you can get it running again," they told him. It sounded like a

SOARING FOR THE KINGDOM

good deal, but he was also concerned that he would not be able to repair the car. Why? The challenge for Rob was the truth that he was dyslexic. In fact he had great difficulty reading anything, let alone complex shop manuals. He was also ADHD which caused him having constant trouble focusing on any one thing for any amount of time. Rob's teachers told his parents they thought his disability could very likely prevent him from graduating from high school without significant changes in his behavior.

But Rob accepted the repair challenge. It took him working for the next two years with friends, and his parents reading to him from the manuals when the topic was complex. He also struggled through the manuals himself, often reading late into the night to make sense of the words in front of him. It was not an easy two years. He nearly gave up dozens of times, especially in the first year. He would cry and throw the manuals across the room or bang his tools on the ground in frustration.

But then halfway through the first year, something began to click for Rob. He successfully replaced the brakes and many of the basic parts and systems. He learned to do the simple things first — before challenging himself with the more advanced, experienced mechanic-level jobs.

With each success, like changing the oil, tuning the engine, replacing all the hoses, and detailing the car (cleaning), his confidence grew.

Once he had all the simple, non-skilled jobs completed, he spent an entire week learning how to replace the clutch. After that, he spent an entire two months dropping and repairing the transmission. He then went on to learn how to diagnose the electrical issues the car had. He spent every spare minute after school and an entire two summers immersed in his car. By his 16th birthday in October, he had the car running and looking beautiful. At the vehicle inspection, he cried when his car passed and was certified roadworthy.

Spiritual Nourishment

His parents were proud of him, not just for fixing the car, but for sticking with the process and learning all he had to learn to do it. His reading comprehension increased tenfold. His attention span was four times what it had been. He was more mature and managed his money better since the cost of parts came out of his allowance and his part-time job mowing lawns. With all the time and effort Rob had put into the car repair, he drove very carefully so he wouldn't wreck it. He kept the car in a portable garage in his parent's yard and kept it immaculately clean all the time. Rob didn't just have the working sports car of his dreams. Rob was a "new man" in the changes he'd undergone while fixing the car.

What Rob had learned was that anything worth having is worth working for. **His time spent in the shop manuals and how-to books was what enabled the changes in Rob.** Not only was he reading and learning all about cars — and his car — but he was subconsciously learning patience and other skills. The entire family learned that if you are motivated enough, you will do "almost anything to achieve your goal."

We tend to think that God limits Himself to spiritual challenges in our lives and is unconcerned with our "day-to-day" ordinary challenges and events. But He tells us, "Anything is possible," and He means it. Christ tells His disciples in Matthew 17:20, " ... for truly I say to you, if you have faith the size of a mustard seed, you will say to this mountain, 'Move from here to there,' and it will move, and nothing will be impossible to you." He says, "Nothing will be impossible."

He repeats this truth throughout the book of Matthew. In Matthew 20:21, He says, "Truly I say to you, if you have faith and do not doubt, you will not only do what was done to the fig tree, but even if you say to this mountain, 'Be taken up and cast into the sea,' it will happen." I think He's making a clear, strong point. Believe. Have Faith. And ... trust God and you can do anything, change anything,

SOARING FOR THE KINGDOM

and become anything. He means, of course, anything in His will and according to His laws and principles.

How motivated are you to change, to follow God, to SOAR for the Kingdom of Heaven? Believers can learn a lesson from Rob when it comes to studying anything we want to learn, master, and implement — especially the Word of God. First Peter 2:2 talks about new believers seeking the milk of God's Word:

"As newborn babes, desire the sincere milk of the word, that ye may grow thereby." Before Rob could repair the car's transmission, he had to learn how to use his tools, and how to think like a mechanic. He needed his confidence in himself and the manuals to be strong before he tackled complex jobs. He was "desiring the milk" or the very basics of car repair. Only when he understood the basics and learned how to use the tools and how to study, could he move into the "meat" or the more complex aspects of car repair.

He needed experience working on his car, having success, and understanding how the entire car worked. He didn't just change the oil. He learned what the oil did, why it was important, and how it affected the engine. The four corners of the SOAR foundation and the six aspects you build upon that foundation will do for you what Rob's shop manual and efforts did for him. He thought he was just fixing a car, but the process he went through — building a foundation of knowledge — changed his entire life.

When you study the Word of God, implement the teachings, and continue to study the Bible in more and more sophisticated ways, your heart will transform and your spirit will change. Your mind, the way you think, act, and see the world and people around you will change. God will see to that. It's being in the Word of God that allows God to transform us.

God's divine power has given us everything we need for life and godliness, and transformation. In 2 Peter 1:3-11, we read, " *His divine power has granted to us all things that pertain to life and godliness, through the knowledge of Him who called us to[3] His own glory and excellence, by which He has granted to us His precious and very great promises, so that through them you may become partakers of the divine nature, having escaped from the corruption that is in the world because of sinful desire. For this very reason, make every effort to supplement your faith with virtue, and virtue with knowledge, and knowledge with self-control, and self-control with steadfastness, and steadfastness with godliness, and godliness with brotherly affection, and brotherly affection with love. For if these qualities are yours and are increasing, they keep you from being ineffective or unfruitful in the knowledge of our Lord Jesus Christ. For whoever lacks these qualities is so nearsighted that he is blind, having forgotten that he was cleansed from his former sins. Therefore, brothers, be all the more diligent to confirm your calling and election, for if you practice these qualities, you will never fall. For in this way there will be richly provided for you an entrance into the eternal kingdom of our Lord and Savior Jesus Christ."*

The Bible states that *transformation* means *"change or renewal from a life that no longer conforms to the ways of the world to one that pleases God." ("Do not be conformed to this world but be transformed by the renewal of your mind, that by testing you may discern what is the will of God, what is good and acceptable and perfect" (Romans* 12:2).

Our physical and spiritual transformation begins with the gospel message of Christ which brings us salvation. From there, God expects us to continue to abide in His Word as He continues to transform us as we grow in both head and heart knowledge of God.

WHAT IS SPIRITUAL NOURISHMENT?

Spiritual nourishment means "feeding the soul." Craving pure "spiritual milk" and daily feeding of the Word is a very important metaphor for healthy spiritual growth. I don't know anyone who

SOARING FOR THE KINGDOM

doesn't recognize when they're hungry! When we're hungry what do we do? We stand in front of the refrigerator and try to decide what it is we really want to eat. We *recognize our cravings* for certain kinds of foods and then we take action to find and eat that food. If we do that on a physical level, how much more important is it to do on a spiritual level?

Peter describes believers "craving the pure spiritual milk of God," in a way people at the time understood. Milk is a powerful symbol in most cultures. It is the fluid of eternal life. It is connected to life, fertility, and abundance. It is the first human diet. Without milk at birth to nourish it, a baby soon withers and dies.

The promised land was described as having milk and honey flowing freely. That wasn't just a random description. Milk is deeply connected with life itself and symbolizes life. It's no wonder the Bible references the Word of God as spiritual milk and nourishment. Honey is also used metaphorically and symbolically to convey a deeper spiritual truth or idea. Can you see how God wants to nourish us through His Word so we can grow? It makes sense that "Spiritual Nourishment[1]" to build our spiritual self is the first corner of the foundation we build upon.

Christ described "drinking the water of life," and referred to His body as bread. Throughout the New Testament, God's Word is described as "milk and meat." You can't feed yourself by watching other people talk about God's word. You have to be IN the Word yourself, reading the Bible, not just hearing it ... In fact, the Bereans (a Protestant sect following former Scottish Presbyterian minister John Barclay) were encouraged to search the Word daily to see if what the disciples said was true.

"Now, *the Bereans were more noble-minded than the Thessalonians, for they received the message with great eagerness and examined the Scriptures every day to see if these teachings were true.*" (Acts 17:11)

Spiritual Nourishment

Rob had dozens of shop manuals that explained his car. We have the 66 books of the Bible that explain us, God, God's will, and plans for man. Just as Rob learned how all the systems of a car work together to transform a non-working car into a working one, we must learn how God's Word and all our systems work to transform us into Godly men and women.

The Bible is a believer's "shop manual." It teaches us about our Maker and Creator. It teaches us about who we are, how we work, and how best to ensure we operate according to what God's plan for us is.

The "milk" of the word is the basic gospel message, and the easily digested truths and concepts Jesus Christ shared with His disciples and the world. The "meat" of the Bible are the books, passages, and spiritual truths that take us time, experience, and study to understand.

When you open the Bible to study it, you have come into the presence of God. You're reading God's Word — His personal communication to you. Every minute or hour you spend reading God's Word isn't just reading. It's a minute or hour you're spending in the very presence of God Himself (Ephesians 6:10). If you think back to meeting your spouse or your first love, you may remember how much you thought of them, or dreamed of the time you'd be together again. Nothing could keep you from them. And if you couldn't be together physically, you were together in your heart and minds until you could be by their side. When you realize that God is real and alive and not just a "concept," your entire life will change. You'll long to be in His Word or hearing it read.

Our love grows and matures, and we transform mentally, emotionally, and even physically with each moment, we spend with the people and things we love. This is also true when we spend time with God in His Word!

If we immerse ourselves in the Bible as Rob immersed himself in his car, we will find ourselves being transformed by both the Word and Spirit of God We will realize our time and effort spent being with God is transforming us and introducing us to who our Creator truly is.

Jesus is the living Word (John 1:14). *"The Word became flesh and made his dwelling among us. We have seen his glory, the glory of the one and only Son, who came from the Father, full of grace and truth."* When Jesus walked out of His tomb, He was risen. He was no longer dead, but alive. He's still alive. And so is His Word!

> *"For the Word of God is alive and active. Sharper than any double-edged sword, it penetrates even to dividing soul and spirit, joints and marrow; it judges the thoughts and attitudes of the heart."*
>
> *— Matthew 4:4*

One of the most difficult concepts for new (or older) Christians to grasp is that the Bible isn't a fantasy or just another book. It is alive. Until you get it inside you by reading it, meditating upon it, and putting what you learn into practice, it doesn't become a part of you. God can't work through you if the talents, gifts, and wisdom of His Word aren't a part of you.

By the time Rob had his car running and he was driving it, he knew more about the car than he could share with anyone. He had become intimately involved with the sounds it made, how it handled, why it handled as it did, and what it was capable of. He "knew" the car inside and out because he engaged with it. He thought about it and reflected how to fix things, and was hands-on with the car. When it made a noise, he knew what was making the noise. Often his passengers would ask, "What noise?" when he asked if they "heard that."

Spiritual Nourishment

When we spend time in the Word, we become intimately involved with God. We learn to hear His voice; sense His pleasure and displeasure. We know Him in a way no one can because they are not us. They'll have their own relationship, but the one we have with God is unique. At some point in time, you will understand what Jesus meant when He said, *"It is written: 'Man shall not live on bread alone, but on every word that comes from the mouth of God.'"* There will come a time — usually when you least expect it — that you will set aside physical food and be satisfied with spiritual food. You just want the Word so much that your physical appetite no longer matters. This can happen as you spend more time in the Word, or as you fast, or when you really need His comfort. It's something I can't explain, but you'll know it when you experience it!

Speaking of the Word as food and nourishment, we can't drink milk (the Bible's basics) and expect to grow to maturity. That's not how things work. We can't just jump into the meat of the Bible without understanding the Bible's basics first And we can't simply watch others ingest milk without drinking it ourselves if we expect to grow.

For instance, no matter how much I watch people cook, bake, sew, run, lift weights or work on their cars, I'm never going to learn how to do anything unless I jump in and do it, too — becoming hands-on. Listening to sermons, going to Sunday School, and hearing others talk about what they learned from the Bible are great opportunities to grow and do benefit us, but they are only a part of our growth. Until I sit down with the Bible, open it up and read it, and learn to study it, I am never going to be fully, spiritually nourished. And while the milk of the Bible is filling, you can't just drink milk the rest of your life and be satisfied, let alone grow and mature. To be a complete Christian, ready to soar, you must have full maturity. 2 Timothy 3:15-17 says, " ... and how from infancy you have known the Holy Scriptures, which can make you wise for salvation through faith in Christ Jesus.[16] All Scripture is God-breathed and is useful for teaching, rebuking, correcting, and training in righteousness,[17] so that the servant of God may be thoroughly equipped for every good work."

Even small babies begin to reach for solid food when milk no longer satisfies them. Some part of them knows they need something more substantial to grow physically. How do you begin to study the scriptures?

WHY IS IT IMPORTANT TO SEEK SPIRITUAL NOURISHMENT?

Physical nourishment enables our bodies to grow. It feeds our muscles, our organs, our entire body. Without nourishment, we will quickly die. **Spiritual nourishment** does the same for our spiritual body. It feeds our soul and spirit and keeps us connected to God. It strengthens our spirit and gives us energy. But spiritual nourishment does something else, it alters our mind, our heart, and our soul, and puts us into a state of mind where we can hear God speak to us.

The Word of God is not like any other book on earth. It is the *living* Word of God, and it changes us, strengthens us, and speaks to us on levels no other book can. In fact, non-believers literally cannot understand the Word of God as a believer can. *"For the message of the cross is foolishness to those who are perishing, but to us who are being saved, it is the power of God ... For since in the wisdom of God, the world through its wisdom did **not** know him, God was pleased through the **foolishness** of what was preached to save those who believe."* — 1 Corinthians 1:18

When we become believers, we are instantly changed. The scales fall from our eyes and hearts in preparation for our study of God's Word. God begins to speak to us, and we begin to experience Him like we never have before. It's a mystery, but a reality.

Spiritual Nourishment

The Word of God strengthens our heart, mind, and soul. Seeking spiritual nourishment begins with establishing a **quiet time** with God, meeting with Him every day to worship, praise, learn, and be with Him through prayer (talking with God) and reading His Word.

HOW TO HAVE A QUIET TIME

Everyone has their own way of having a quiet time. The details don't matter as long as it works for you. This is what I do:

I find a quiet place where I won't be disturbed. I turn off my cell phone, close the door and gather my Bible, a red pen, a blue pen, and a journal. The blue pen is for what I say to God, and the red pen is for what God says to me.

How you structure your quiet time with God is up to you, but it should include:

Worship. Begin by focusing on who God is and His unconditional love, His Word, and how holy His presence is. This is your time to meet with the Father! Even Jesus met regularly with His Father. Jesus would often withdraw to a quiet place to pray. "Very early in the morning, while it was still dark, Jesus got up, left the house, and went off to a solitary place, where He prayed." (Mark 1:35.) Jesus, who was the Son of God, felt it necessary to meet with Him daily. Why wouldn't we?

Gratitude. This is part of praise. Keep a gratitude journal for all things you're grateful for and especially for answered prayers — no matter how small.

Study. Bible study sounds like homework at first, doesn't it? But Bible study is simply getting to know Jesus' story. When you meet someone new, you want to know about them, who their family is, where they came from, what they do for a living, where they live, and any details you can discover to help you understand them better. The

SOARING FOR THE KINGDOM

Bible is how we learn Christ's "story." Where was He born? How did He grow up? Did you know Jesus had brothers and sisters? Yes! He did. Matthew 13:55–56 mentions James, Joseph/Joses, Judas/Jude, and Simon as half-brothers of Jesus, the son of Mary. The same verses also mention unnamed half-sisters of Jesus. Don't you want to know what roles they played in His life?

Enjoy. If you have a spouse, or child, or close friend, don't you meet with them every day? It might be a phone call if you're not living together, or an email, or text. You just enjoy connecting with them even if it's over something normal or part of your day. The key point is you share your day with them. God wants us to share our day with Him, too. Yes, He knows all that has happened to us, what we're thinking, feeling, wanting, and where we're hurting. But it's the connection He craves. If you have a child, you "know" what they're doing or about. But that doesn't stop you from wanting to hear them tell you about their day or ask for your help. God craves our attention and love. He wants to help, to protect, and share, and teach. And He does that through His Word.

Spiritual Nourishment

TIPS:

- Make your daily quiet time a priority. Don't let distractions pull you away from it.
- Pick a time and quiet place to spend this time in. Be consistent in seeking God there.
- Include prayer and worship to begin and end each time — even if you only spend 5-10 minutes in study to begin with.
- Ask for guidance and insights from the Holy Spirit.
- Write down prayer requests, insights or revelations, or questions in a journal. If you have a question, write it down and leave room for an answer later.
- Whatever insights, questions, or thoughts come to you to explore. Write them down.
- Have an agenda or plan for your reading. Be working on understanding something or look for guidance and help in developing something about yourself.
- Don't try to read and comprehend more than two-to-three chapters a day.
- Don't go to the Bible trying to prove or disprove something. Humans are prone to take things out of context when they do this.
- Start with the New Testament rather than the Old Testament. People who start reading the New Testament first are more likely to read the entire Bible than those who start with the Old Testament first.
- Read the Gospels (Matthew, Mark, Luke, John) first. Once you read a book, reread it and reread it until you know it by heart (Over time! Not all in one sitting!)

SOARING FOR THE KINGDOM

ACTION ITEMS

- Get a blank notebook or journal to use for your quiet time to record prayer requests, notes, and questions you have about what you're reading. This notebook should be solely for your quiet time insights, notes, and prayer requests/questions.
- Set a time for having a quiet time. Begin with 15 minutes of prayer and reading.
- Decide on three spiritual goals for yourself, such as spending at least 90 minutes in the Word each week, reading the Gospel of Matthew, Mark, Luke, or John by the end of 30 days, etc.

Chapter 2

Organize Your Life

O — Organize your life, to pursue an ordered path.

A God of Order

Have you ever been to a nice hotel or restaurant? When you walked into the business was it clean? Did it smell good? Were the beds made? Were the towels fresh? Were the tables in the restaurant wiped clean, and was the silverware spotless and shining? Were the waiters neatly dressed and clean?

Have you ever been to a friend's house where everything was put away, orderly, clean, and smelled fresh? How did it feel to walk into these places? Now try to think of walking into a house or business where there was trash on the floor and dirty pots and pans in the sink. Maybe there were crumbs on the table, the trash cans were overflowing, and it smelled like rotting food or mold. Which space made you feel more calm and relaxed? I'm going to guess the places that were clean and orderly made you feel calmer, more relaxed, and safe. Even if our own homes or offices are messy and disorderly, we prefer orderliness and cleanliness, and so do our bodies.

We are hardwired to function better when there is order and organization in our lives. That is the state we prefer. Some of us, due to upbringing or other circumstances, may not live in the cleanest or most orderly of spaces, but very, very few mentally healthy people will willingly stay in a cluttered or disordered home unless they are forced to for health, disability, or other reasons.

Keeping things clean and organized not only feels good, but it's also good for you, and science can prove it. A study led by associate professor NiCole R. Keith, Ph.D., research scientist, and professor at Indiana University, found that people with clean houses are healthier than people with messy houses.[1] According to Indiana University, "Keith and her colleagues tracked the physical health of 998 African Americans between the ages of 49 and 65, a demographic known to be at an increased risk for heart disease. Participants who kept their homes clean were healthier and more active than those who didn't. House cleanliness was even more of a predictor for physical health than neighborhood walkability."[2]

God is a God of order. If you look at nature, you'll see a phenomenon called "The Golden Mean." It's a mathematical expression that describes the universe. The **"golden mean"** is the desirable middle between two extremes — one of excess and the other of deficiency. It is life, nature, creatures, and the world around us, balanced. Everything from our DNA to the stars and planets is ordered and organized. Everything has a purpose. Part of that purpose is renewal. From rain to floods, to fires and natural disasters, and even global warming or change, the earth is designed to clean itself, and our bodies to rebuild themselves from the inside out, replacing blood cells, skin cells, and every organ in our body every seven years. I find it interesting that God created the week to have seven days, His jubilee years are seven, and the soil in farmers' fields

Organize Your Life

is supposed to lie fallow, with no crops, every seventh year. There's something to that kind of structure and order I won't go into here, but I do find it more than coincidental, don't you?

God has even designed a system in our bodies called *autophagy*. It's the body's way of cleaning out damaged cells, to regenerate newer, healthier cells. "Auto" means self, and "phage" means eat. So, the literal meaning of autophagy is **"self-eating**."[3] "Self-eating" may sound disgusting, but it's amazing. Autophagy is a self-preservation mechanism through which the body can remove dysfunctional cells and recycle parts of them for cellular repair and cleaning. We stimulate this process when we fast — yes, a God-designed and required process that stimulates the autophagy process. Scientists are discovering that God has built in this "reset button" to create order in our systems. It's believed that autophagy can reverse diabetes, and even cure cancer — all through simply fasting.[4]

Earth as we know it now is not as perfect as the Garden of Eden because when Mankind fell, sin entered the world and impacted nature as well. But, if you look at everything from the dimensions of dolphins to the arms of starfish, plant structures, the strands of our DNA, the patterns in seashells, and more, it's all structured according to the mathematics of the golden mean.

God is holy and perfect, and there is no room for chaos or disorder in His universe. *"For God is not a God of disorder but of peace."* (1 Corinthians 14:33)

When Paul wrote this letter, he was writing to the Corinthian church. It was a letter rebuking them for the disorder and chaos in the church at Corinth. He wasn't just "perturbed." He was angry! He appears to have been so angry over this dispute with one man in the church, he could not even travel to Corinth to meet with members of the church face-to-face. The disagreement that made Paul so angry was with one incestuous man, a man Paul already told the church to expel from the congregation.[5]

SOARING FOR THE KINGDOM

While we might think the believers and Christians of Paul's time were more "spiritual" and together than we are today, they weren't. Even though the very disciples of Christ were teaching and leading them, they were a chaotic mess. Their worship services were out of control, and worse, they were in such chaos, that nonbelievers and outsiders considered them "mad" (1 Corinthians 14:23). They were not the best witnesses for Christ.

If you read 1 Corinthians, you may find that Paul addresses many of the same chaotic situations, sins, and problems at Corinth as we do in the church today:

- Celibacy within marriage (7:1–7)
- Chaos in worship, with many of the believers speaking in tongues and competing voices (Chapter 14)
- Christians married to one another asking about divorce (7:8–11, 39)
- Christians married to non-believers asking about divorce (7:12–16)
- Concerns about women praying and prophesying in immodest ways (11:2–16)
- Denials of the bodily resurrection of Jesus and of Christians (15:1–58)
- Idolatry (8:1–11:1)
- Incest (5:1–13)
- Inequality in the communal meal (11:17–34)
- Questions surrounding marriage and remarriage (7:25–40)
- Lawsuits against other believers (6:1–11)
- Prostitution (6:12–21)

While many of us tend to think of order and organization in terms of items rather than spiritual or Biblical terms and events, chaos and order can be found in everything. When our house or office, or room is "ordered," it is neat, tidy, and clean. Things are easy to find, and

18

Organize Your Life

everything in the room has a place. When we are in order spiritually, we are in the Word, are calmer and focused on Christ, and are maturing.

When we think of order and organization in terms of people, we may envision a sort of military or minimalist orientation. Clothes are clean and pressed, shoes are shined, people are clean and of a clear mind with a purpose, goals, and actions. Their environment is orderly and tidy as well.

God is a creator of order. He created the universe in an orderly sequence so each day would build and run on the day before. He didn't create fish before He created water. He created the sun, moon, and stars before He created the time and seasons. The heavenly bodies operated with preciseness in a consistent, predictable way before other processes were added.

> *"For in six days, the Lord made heaven and earth, the sea, and all that is in them, and rested on the seventh day. Therefore, the Lord blessed the Sabbath day and made it holy."*
>
> *— Exodus 20:11*

> *"It is a sign forever between me and the people of Israel that in six days the Lord made heaven and earth, and on the seventh day he rested and was refreshed."*
>
> *— Genesis 31:17*

> *"And God saw everything that he had made, and behold, it was very good. And there was evening and there was morning, the sixth day."*
>
> *— Genesis 1:31*

SOARING FOR THE KINGDOM

"And God said, 'Let there be lights in the expanse of the heavens to separate the day from the night. And let them be for signs and for seasons, and for days and years,[15] and let them be lights in the expanse of the heavens to give light upon the earth." And it was so.[16] And God made the two great lights — the greater light to rule the day and the lesser light to rule the night — and the stars.[17] And God set them in the expanse of the heavens to give light on the earth,[18] to rule over the day and over the night, and to separate the light from the darkness. And God saw that it was good."

— Genesis 1:14-18

When God created man, He created an orderly body where each organ receives blood and oxygen and is interdependent on other organs. The lungs receive oxygen and send it to the blood, and the heart pumps oxygen-enriched blood through organs designed to receive it. Every organ has a job to do and interacts with other organs in a perfect flow of life.

Our brains regulate our temperature, appetites, organs, pain, respiration, and thoughts and feelings. Most of what keeps us alive minute-to-minute is automatic. We don't have to think about how to walk, talk, digest our food, make new cells, and shed old ones. We don't have to think about what we need to do to sleep, fight off diseases, or make new blood cells. Our bodies are marvels of God's design but are affected by sin and the death Adam and Eve brought onto man and earth when they sinned. But they are ordered. Doctors can treat us because we are so ordered.

Millions of miles of nerves, blood cells, and DNA interact to form who we are. We are walking, talking miracles of God's order and organization.

Organize Your Life

Let's not forget God Himself. We can't comprehend Him, but God is one, three in one Father, Son, and Holy Spirit. All three function in one perfect, orderly, harmony.

Part of how we know God is a God of order is how He created the universe, time, man, and all the creatures on Earth. We know God exists outside of time — the Bible tells us so. Yet, He created time as a way for the universe to mark changes in seasons and time for us. He created time apart from man, in an orderly, sequential manner that man cannot control or alter — although, throughout the centuries, He has tried to.

But time is irrelevant to God because He transcends it. Peter tells his readers that God's perspective on time is far different from mankind's.

> *"But, beloved, do not forget this one thing, that with the Lord one day is as a thousand years and a thousand years as one day."*
>
> — 2 Peter 3:8

God does not count time as we do — which is one of the reasons I think many of us panic when God doesn't answer prayer on our time, but in His perfect timing. He is not limited by time as we are. He's above, outside, and not controlled by time. He sees eternity's past and future all at once. He is above and outside of the sphere of time. He is timeless. A second is no different from an eon; a billion years pass like seconds.

Time is orderly, and sequential and does not vary based on anything mankind can control. Time keeps us orderly and whether we use it or abuse it, we can't change it. Rich or poor, young or old, we all have the same number of hours in a day. The sun will rise and set on schedule no matter what may happen on Earth. Because God is a

SOARING FOR THE KINGDOM

God of order, He keeps everything in motion as He first designed. It is His orderly hand that holds the world in place (Hebrews 1:3; Colossians 1:17).

God deals with us in orderly ways. He answers prayers at exactly the right time, which may seem to us like "the last possible minute." Yet we should know better. God is a planner. He sent His Son, Jesus Christ, into the world at just the right time, and let His people know, hundreds of years before Christ's arrival, exactly when and where He would arrive and the signs to look for (Galatians 4:4).

God does not spring things on us to catch us unaware. He gives us notice and tells us when things are going to happen. *"Surely the Lord GOD does nothing unless He reveals His secret to His servants the prophets."* Christ's birth was not a surprise to the Magi or King David. David knew long before the time Jesus would be born, and he left an inheritance to the Magi for them to take to Christ. For those who love, follow, and worship God, nothing comes as a surprise. He has given His followers prophecy to prepare them for what lies ahead. Although the world now appears to be in chaos, with "wars and rumors of wars," earthquakes and volcanoes, and pestilences, famines, and disasters, God told us all this would happen. He told us Israel would become a nation in a day.

> *"Who has ever heard of such things? Who has ever seen things like this? Can a country be born in a day, or a nation be brought forth in a moment? Yet no sooner is Zion in labor than she gives birth to her children. Do I bring to the moment of birth and not give delivery?" says the Lord. "Do I close up the womb when I bring to delivery?" says your God. "Rejoice with Jerusalem and be glad for her, all you who love her; rejoice greatly with her, all you who mourn over her"* (Isaiah 66:8-10).

> *"Never in the history of the world had such a thing happened before — but God keeps His Word. As definitely foretold in Isaiah and in*

Organize Your Life

Ezekiel 37:21, 22, Israel became a recognized nation, actually "born in one day."

God is so ordered and organized He even gave His laws and festivals to His people to practice and learn about ahead of time so they'd be ready when Christ arrived. A patient Father, God gave His people His laws and showed them how to approach Him. God didn't spring the idea of a Savior on the world. He spent centuries patiently preparing the world in an orderly fashion (Mark 14:49; John 3:16–18; 5:39).

Man was created in "God's image." He created us as triune beings — spirit, soul, and body. He also created us to think in orderly ways, to reason, to be wise, and to consider all aspects of a matter before acting. It's not His fault we fail to do what He taught in His Word. He longs for us to be orderly and organized and to seek Him and learn to know Him through His Word. When we become more ordered and organized, we become more like God. And the more we become like Him, the more we understand Him and the closer we become to Him.

God's order and organization are so ingrained in us that even if companies and people don't believe in God, they believe in the order He hardwired into us. There's a reason why the military and military schools start a student or recruit's life with learning how to order and organize everything. From their toothbrushes, and making their beds, to polishing their shoes and even how they sit, walk, stand, eat, and sleep, there is a structure every soldier, sailor, and Marine learns to follow. The military knows that to run smoothly and effectively, things must be ordered, and people must be organized and follow the same structure and policies as those around them.

Even if you aren't in the military, you know your university, job, or office has policies to ensure order is maintained. You may have some leeway in how you do some things, but successful businesses are organized and ordered.

One company comes to mind when I think about order — UPS. UPS ships 5 billion packages a year.[6] The company is so aware of how critical order and organization are, they used to train all their drivers to carry their keys on their ring fingers before switching to keyless fobs in 2011. They also don't let UPS trucks turn left to save time spent idling in turn lanes. Routes are laid out, so drivers only turn right when possible. They shave seconds off their delivery time that way.[7] From how they receive, ship, drive and deliver packages, there is no other company more organized and orderly than UPS. Sorting and juggling, and a lack of planning cause us to lose time, focus, and purpose.

If companies, corporations, and our military can develop self-discipline, order, and organization, why should we, as believers and followers of the greatest organizer of all time, God, do any less? God, the Father delights in helping each of His children turn their weakness into strength and that includes getting organized. Your home may not be organized. You may not be organized. Your desk, your financial concerns, or your car may not be clean or organized. Those things are a reflection of the inner man or woman. With God's help, you can change — starting with your spiritual life. As your quiet time and your spiritual life become a discipline, you'll begin to notice a desire and the ability to organize and structure the rest of your life as well.

Biblical Examples of Order

The Bible consists of 66 books written by more than 40 men over 1,500 years. And yet, the order, consensus, and details of the Bible never contradict themselves or give us anything but a divinely ordered manuscript that never contradicts itself, as inspired by God. God didn't dictate the Bible, but He inspired the men who wrote it,

Organize Your Life

using the men's unique personalities. And while in America, we take the seven-day week for granted, not every country in the world does. As far as we know, in all the ancient world, there was no seven-day calendar cycle except for the Jewish week, which existed at the very beginning of the monarchical period in Israel [approximately 1000 B.C.] and perhaps even earlier than that. The seven-day week also happens to correspond with our circadian rhythms and with God's original design.

According to *The Amazing Seven Day Cycle* by Kenneth Westby, "Both Christianity and Islam inherited the seven-day week from the Jews. Both established worship days separate from the Jews: Sunday for the Christians, and Friday for the Muslims — both days touching the original Sabbath. These three religions, with their three worship days clustering together, have played key historical roles in bringing the beat of a seven-day week to all the world."[8] Scientists have discovered that these innate, autonomous, seven-day cycles are hardwired into the very building blocks of plant and animal life. These newly found sevens, or "septans," also lie buried in us humans — deep in our metabolic, hormonal, and neuronal networks where they cannot be altered.

Over the centuries, man, including the Romans, Greeks, Alexander the Great, and in modern times, Stalin, France, Russia, and others, have tried to eliminate the seven-day week in an attempt to destroy Christianity and Judaism, but have failed miserably. Now, chronobiology (the study of how living beings handle time) has discovered there are five major rhythms that beat in our bodies to ensure our health and happiness.

Our daily or circadian rhythm (from the Latin for "around a day") is the easiest to detect and measure. We are born with our own set of circadian rhythms that, in time, become synchronized with our environment. Our rhythms vary slightly from individual to individual (23.6 hours, 24.3 hours, 25.4 hours, etc.) and 12. They usually

SOARING FOR THE KINGDOM

shorten as we age. Most, if not all, of the millions of daily functions that occur in our bodies are organized within some rhythmic system dictated by the seven-day cycle. Some bodily tasks occur quickly in seconds, minutes, or hours, and others slowly over months.[9]

When God created the Earth, He created order

Order and organization weren't afterthoughts. God had a plan for His universe, people, and creations on earth. No detail was left to chance or whim. We may think God only gets involved in the "big things" like wars and presidents, kings, and nations. But no. God is so organized He has numbered the hairs on our heads, and He knows when a sparrow falls to earth. He knows every human being who was ever born before they were conceived.

He has set a time for our birth and a date for our death. He is involved in every aspect of our lives. When Moses struggled to deal with and settle the disputes of the Hebrews during the Exodus, God intervened, giving him advice on how to rule through Jethro, Moses' father-in-law. Jethro told Moses to stop wearing himself out, trying to settle every dispute in camp. He told Moses he should establish a multi-tied judicial system, effectively selecting and placing "men of truth" as leaders and judges of thousands, hundreds, the fifties, and tens. It's a system much like our modern name court system, with the "top court in the land" being the Supreme Court (Exodus 18:13-26).

When Christ sent out His disciples, He sent them in teams of two and gave them detailed, organized instructions on what they were to wear and how they were to conduct themselves (Mark 6:7).

Before Jesus fed the crowd of more than five 5,000 women, and children, He had them form into groups so that the distribution and the collecting of food would be orderly. Otherwise, chaos would have ensued as the people rushed to get what they probably imagined were limited rations (Matthew 15:35). Decision-making, assignment of

Organize Your Life

space, the accomplishment of tasks, and clear lines of communication are thus ordered with one goal in mind — that our lives and environment might be so composed as to give maximum freedom so we can SOAR in our Kingdom assignments.

When organizing our homes or offices, give order to policies and structures that benefit and bless the people in your sphere of influence.

Think of your process of organization similar to a symphony. A symphony has four sections, consisting of woodwinds, brass, percussion, and strings. If you've ever attended a symphony, you've probably noticed that the symphony orchestra is organized according to the sections. Each section has been appropriately placed, so when the symphony begins, the conductor knows precisely where each unit is and when to bring each section in. The sections' organizing/placement creates a harmonious sound when all parts are played together.

Because each section is appropriately placed, the conductor quickly knows when, where, and how to tell each section when to come in.

When all the sections/parts of our lives are organized, we will create harmony with our time, energy, and relationships. We must analyze and appropriately place each piece in our lives to know where to go when we need to find something. A harmonious life is a low-stress life. It has been scientifically proven that with less stress, we are healthier and happier. We are the conductor of our lives.

Answer these questions in 5 seconds or less:

- Do your keys have a designated place?
- Are your essential papers in a designated place and organized alphabetically or numerically, depending on what type of documents?

- When you go to your closet, can you easily find your clothes for the day or season, or does thinking of your closet cause stress?
- Do you have a systematic approach to grocery shopping?
- Do you know to the penny what your financial budget is? Remember, a budget is a road map to get you from point a to point b and what adjustments are needed to help you get there.
- If God were to ask your provider how much is short in your budget, could you answer Him and provide financial documentation to support your request? Remember, He told us to ask, and we will receive. Again, do you know in 5 seconds or fewer how much to ask?
- Do you have a morning routine during school season and when school season is out? Alternatively, is everyone running around frantically in the mornings looking for things, thus causing our family relationships to start on a wrong note?

If you cannot answer these questions in 5 seconds or fewer, some organizing is needed.

Organization and an ordered path in my life are essential to function and be effective spiritually, mentally, emotionally, and physically. One of my most substantial spiritual gifts is administration. I used the tools and techniques shared in this book regularly, and when life gets busy and I derail and need to put the harmony back in my life.

GOAL SETTING

Goals are dreams with a deadline. But attainable goals are organized and orderly goals. We either move ahead or fall behind. There is no middle ground, no straddling a fence, or waffling about our decision. Christ, Himself said he hated "lukewarm" commitments and vomited

Organize Your Life

the lukewarm believer from His mouth. If you've ever been with someone who couldn't commit to anything, you'll understand how He felt. There is nothing more frustrating than someone who can't make up their mind, or who can't commit to a direction. No matter how grand, noble, or Christ-worthy a desire or dream is, if it can't be measured, has no deadline, and has no organized plan, it's useless. To be achievable, goals must be S.M.A.R.T. goals.

- Specific — Proverbs 16:3
- Measurable — Hebrew 6:10
- Achievable — Phil 3:13,14
- Relevant — Matthew 22:37-40
- Time-Bound — 1 Chr. 12:32; Acts 20:24

Specific = The goal must be specific and measurable. It's not enough to say, "My goal is to be a success." The goal must be specific. How will you know you are a success? I have several goals, including writing a book, completing my degree, and owning a business. When setting a specific goal, ask questions like:

- What objective needs to be accomplished? For example, "What classes do I need to take to complete my degree? Or write my book?"
- Who is responsible for what steps?
- What steps do I need to take to achieve this goal? What do I need to do next?

Measurable = Having specific goals and plans is a start, but the critical aspect of a SMART goal is the numbers. What will my degree cost? How many semesters of classes will I need? How much time will it take me to attend class, study, and achieve my goals? Making your goals measurable is important, if not critical to your success.

Achievable = Are my goals achievable? Can I reach them with the time, talent, skills, and resources I have available to me? Am I "aiming too high" or being unrealistic? Be honest with yourself. Make sure you can achieve your goal given your finances, time, talent, skills, and energy. No matter how noble the goal, don't bite off more than you can chew.

Relevant = You must see a benefit in setting this goal. No one sets a goal for the fun of it. There must be a pay-off or benefit to you for reaching your goal. Is there? Why does this goal matter to you? My education and this book matter to me because they'll help me reach my ultimate goal of owning my own business and helping people one-on-one, teaching, traveling, and speaking. While those are all goals I have, I know I must focus on each step as I work towards my ultimate goals.

Time-Bound = What is my timeline for achieving my goals? Is it doable? What's the date for completion and what is my deadline? Whether we planned on it or not, most of us finished high school and took some college courses, and others earned advanced degrees, or attended trade school, or landed a job or career. Our parents may have pushed us through high school, but once you were out of high school, did you think about another four years of college or not? If you pursued professional degrees, like law, medicine, engineering, etc., were you prepared to consider the number of years it would take you to complete your training and/or education?

Driven to succeed

The Apostle Paul was driven to succeed, even if it meant killing Christians. While many people think Paul was a monster (including many of his Jewish brethren) it's important to realize Paul (when he was Saul) loved God beyond most. He saw Christianity as a religion that threatened his God, a religion that was intent on corrupting and

Organize Your Life

destroying Judaism. So he set out to destroy the heretics who were threatening the God he'd worshipped his entire life.

His passion for God and Judaism came from his upbringing. He was born a Jew in Tarsus but raised and educated in Jerusalem under Gamaliel, a highly respected rabbi and Jewish scholar. Gamaliel mentored him on the "strict manner of the law of our fathers" (Acts 22:3). Paul was devoted to God; he wasn't shy about letting people know he was a "Jew's Jew," saying, "*If anyone else thinks he has a reason for confidence in the flesh, I have more: circumcised on the eighth day, of the people of Israel, of the tribe of Benjamin, a Hebrew of Hebrews; as to the law, a Pharisee; as to zeal, a persecutor of the church; as to righteousness under the law, blameless*" (Philippians 3:4-6).

The passion Paul once exhibited by killing Christians was transferred into his awakened passion for Christ and the gospel. He spoke of pressing toward the goal for the prize (Phil 3:14) and of running toward a prize. He spoke of disciplining himself to obtain that prize (1 Cor. 9:24, 25). When Paul referenced athletes in his letters, he was referring to the Olympic athletes, the professional athletes of his time. These were men who trained as much or more than the Olympic athletes of our time. These men devoted their lives to their sport as much as Paul devoted his life to Christ. He was deeply committed to God and did not take his goals lightly. He fully intended to run his race and die crossing the finish line if need be.

Paul's goals were God's goals for his life. Yes, God has goals and plans for each one of us, goals He has devised to be for His glory and our best good. He requires us to aim our goals toward the right and eternal things first. "Seek ye first the kingdom of God (Matthew 6:33), thy kingdom come thy will be done on earth as it is in heaven (Matthew 6:10).

SOARING FOR THE KINGDOM

- Biblical guidelines must determine our goals — 1 Corinthians 10:31
- Kingdom goals must come from seeking God for direction — Proverbs 3:5-6
- Kingdom goals must be aligned with the Word of God — 2 Timothy 3:14-17
- Kingdom goals must be in alignment with the mind of God — Phil 2:5-11

Goals — whether a single objective or a lifetime objective — must be written out, and plans considered before you begin a project in order to succeed.

> *"Suppose one of you wants to build a tower. Won't you first sit down and estimate the cost to see if you have enough money to complete it?"*
>
> *— Luke 14:28.*

God is a God of order and process and planning. *"The plans of the diligent lead to profit as surely as haste leads to poverty."*

> *— Proverbs 21:5.*

> *"Commit to the Lord whatever you do, and he will establish your plans."*
>
> *— Proverbs 16:3.*

Allot proper time to complete each task.

Organize Your Life

Objectives for what needs to be done and how you're going to do it are essential. You can devise your own plans without consulting the Lord but be prepared to see them change.

> *"The steps of a good man are[4] ordered by the Lord, And He delights in his way. Though he fall, he shall not be utterly cast down; For the Lord upholds him with His hand."*
>
> — *Psalm 37:23,24; Prov. 16:9.*

Take time and find a space to reflect and evaluate what must be included in your plans and goals.

> *"I have fought a good fight, I have finished my course, I have kept the faith: Henceforth there is laid up for me a crown of righteousness, which the Lord, the righteous judge, shall give me at that day: and not to me only, but unto all them also that love his appearing" (II Timothy 4:7-8).*

The ultimate goal of all Christ-followers is to please God and to:

- Discover His priorities — Matt. 22:36-40
- Study His priorities — Psalms 119:105
- Use His method of evaluating progress — Gal. 6:3,4
- Keep in mind that He promises to help — Phil. 1:6
- Stick with His way of problem-solving — Psalms 37:4-9

Time Management

There is no such thing as time management. We all get 24 hours in a day. We can't gain more time. We can only ensure that how we use our time is efficient and productive. Time management is not about keeping track of your time but instead finding your Kingdom assignment and moving in a direction to accomplish your goals.

SOARING FOR THE KINGDOM

First, acknowledge you have time. God has given each person the same amount of time.

> We err when we let others decide our priorities instead of God and establish our priorities (Romans 12:2).

> Utilizing small bits of time faithfully will equal to great accomplishments (Eccl 9:10).

Devote the evening hours to quiet rest, reflection, and "inner preparation." In other words, prepare and plan for the day ahead and rise early to plan your schedule for the day.

Priorities:

To set priorities is to determine what is important to you and how your time is to be apportioned —who or what takes precedence over different parts of your life.

Scriptures contain guidelines for God's order (Psalms 119:105) that involve:

1. Your relationship with Jesus Christ (Matt. 6:33; Phili. 3.8)
2. Commitment to home life (Gen. 2;24; ps. 127:3; Eph. 5:22, 25;6:4; 1 Tim. 3:2-5; 5:8; 1 Peter 3:7)
3. Service to God through ministries in the church and involvement in the community (Col. 3:17)
4. Responsibility to employer and tasks assigned (1 Thess. 4:11, 12)

Once the Kingdom-appointed criteria are set, you're ready to take on opportunities so you can move forward with the most effective and productive management of time and resources.

Organize Your Life

The best method to accomplish your task is to consider each with prayer (Psalm 19:14). Sometimes you must say "no" as even did Jesus (Luke 4:42,43). Above all else, Kingdom priorities must be determined based on spiritual values and must always overshadow worldly pursuit (2 Cor. 4:18).

Health Benefits of Being Organized

There are a lot of benefits to being organized.

Reduces stress. When we live in clutter or disorganization, we live with stress. Studies show that living with clutter causes stress. How? When we're not organized, we waste time looking for items we can't find, and we waste money buying more items we know we have but can't find. When we can't find things like coats, car keys, files, and shoes, we're often late for our appointments, school, or work. So, being disorganized creates pressure around showing up late and unprepared for work, school, and social events.

Boosts self-confidence. When we're organized, we feel good about ourselves. Instead of saying, "How could I lose my car keys again?" or "I'm not getting anything done," we can say, "It's so much easier to finish things when I have all my tools." We feel good because we're not frustrated with not being able to find what we need to finish or start a project. Studies show that Americans spend 2.5 days a year just looking for their stuff.[10]

Instead of those negative messages you used to hear, like, "Why can't I get anything done?" your inner voice will begin to shout out, "I've got this!" Your self-confidence will soar. You'll feel good about yourself and all of life's possibilities.

It makes you more productive. By knowing where your things "live," it's easier to find them. By not wasting time or getting frustrated with lost items, you can establish routines that let you do more in less time.

SOARING FOR THE KINGDOM

It can save you money. Have you ever bought something you knew you already owned but couldn't find? When your home is organized, there's no longer a need to purchase duplicate items because you can't find the one you own. You can eat out less, purchase fewer items, and not need to duplicate your tools, clothing, and other things.

It saves you time. When you're not walking from room to room or going in circles looking for things, you save time—hours of time over a year.

It enhances creativity. When you're organized, you aren't stressed by visual clutter. That means you've got the energy and peace of mind to be more creative. When you declutter, get organized, and simplify your surroundings, your creativity rises.

You gain clarity and experience a surge of physical and mental energy that opens up opportunities for your creative spark to ignite. This can occur in a craft room, the kitchen, the studio, or even while working on the computer.

- **It helps you adapt**. Whether it's a family emergency, a sick child, or the opportunity to join a friend on an impromptu girls' weekend away, you're much better equipped to adapt to unforeseen circumstances when your day-to-day life is not entirely chaotic.
- **Improves your health**. You have time to focus on eating healthy and exercise.
- **Positions us to help others**. By regularly decluttering our homes, we have multiple opportunities to bless others by donating the items we no longer need.
- **It can improve our relationships**. When we're less stressed, more healthy, and productive, it puts us in a better position to be the best spouse/parent/friend/sibling we can be.

Organize Your Life

ACTION ITEMS

- Clean, declutter and organize a "command station," such as a desk or a corner of your bedroom or kitchen, where you can have quiet time and work on your goals.
- Spend at least one hour this week thinking about your personal and professional goals and writing them down. Pick the most important goal you have for your self and your professional self. "Reverse engineer your goals," and create S.M.A.R.T. goals out of them. Reverse engineering means looking at what you want to achieve, then working backward to determine the steps you'll need to take along the way to achieve that goal.
- Write or type out your goals and post them where you can read them daily.

Chapter 3

Accountable To God And Man

A — Accountable to God and His laws, as well man's laws (Roman 14:12). "So then every one of us shall give account of himself to God."

"Have you eaten from the tree from which I commanded you not to eat?" God asked Adam and Eve. He'd just asked the couple where they were after coming to the garden. Of course, God knew exactly where they were, what they'd done, and what they would say when He questioned them. But the couple needed to be accountable, and He gave them that chance. But they failed. After Adam said he hid from God because he was "naked and ashamed," God asked them more questions. He got right to the point.

In response to Adam's reply, God asked, "Who told you that you were naked? Have you eaten from the tree that I commanded you not to eat from?"

All Adam had to do was say, "Yes, I did. I'm sorry. Forgive me." Maybe Adam would have done that before the fall, but by eating of the tree sin had already entered him. It took only hours, or maybe

Accountable To God And Man

even only minutes, for sin to begin to affect Adam and Eve's thought processes and actions.

Adam said, "The woman you put here with me, gave me some fruit from the tree, and I ate it." Unwilling to be accountable, even when confronted with the truth, Adam could not be honest with God. He knew God loved him, but he just couldn't be honest with Him. Instead, he blamed Eve, *and* brazenly enough, he blamed God. "The woman *YOU* put here with me," Adam said, implying that he would never have done wrong had God not given him Eve as a helpmeet and partner. I wonder sometimes how that made Eve felt. Here was the man God put her with, the protector and helpmate to be by her side, and there he was, throwing her under the bus at the first sign of having to be accountable. But she wasn't that much better.

Then the Lord God said to the woman, "What is this you have done?"

The woman said, "The serpent deceived me, and I ate." Eve was no more willing to be accountable than Adam, blaming the serpent for her disobedience and completely ignoring the fact that she chose to disobey God, deliberately and consciously giving into temptation. *"When the woman saw that the fruit of the tree was **good for** food and pleasing to the eye, and also desirable for gaining wisdom, she took some and ate it."* — Genesis 3:6.

Ever since sin entered the human race, we have not been willing to be accountable for our actions. It's something we've had to learn, and most of us hate learning it until we learn to love God first. If Adam and Eve, who walked and talked with God in the Garden of Eden and knew Him upfront and personally, did not want to be accountable for their decision, how much harder it is for us who don't know God well?

The other thing this story tells us is that God sees all and knows all. He watches everything we do and knows everything we think. He

SOARING FOR THE KINGDOM

knows what we're going to do before we have even thought about a thing. Yet, as clear as He makes this fact to us in His Word, many of us believe we can still hide our thoughts, actions, and temptations from Him. We can't! He knew us before we were even conceived! He knows the number of hairs on your head, and the number of tears in the bottle of tears He collects from us.

We are still influenced by our guilt, sin, and fear of being held accountable for our decisions and actions. We think we can somehow avoid God, just as Adam and Eve did! So many of us find ways of avoiding accountability and think we have succeeded in throwing God off the track. Or we take minimal accountability for our decisions, and like Adam and Eve, blame others or bring in others who can share in the blame, or who allow us to claim, "plausible deniability." No one likes to be held accountable in the world's sense of the term. Even if we do claim responsibility under man's definition, it rarely feels good. I can understand how Adam and Eve must have felt ashamed and embarrassed.

There's an old saying I heard a while back, "If you can't do the time, don't do the crime." It's a way of saying, "If you can't accept responsibility for your actions, don't act." Yet, the more I thought about accountability and studied what it truly means, I discovered the accountability God expects is different from the accountability the world expects. The world, and Satan, are all about guilting us into lying, denying, and avoiding responsibility for our actions and decisions.

But how does God want us to be accountable? How does He view accountability? According to Merriam-Webster Dictionary online, accountability is, "the quality or state of being accountable; an obligation or willingness to accept responsibility or to account for one's actions." God's definition of accountability comes from Romans 14:12: "So then each one of us shall give an account of himself to God." The way the world defines accountability and the way God

40

Accountable To God And Man

defines it are two separate things, yet I believe God expects us to be accountable to both man and God. Just as Jesus said in Mark 12:17, "Render unto Caesar the things that are Caesar's, and the things that are God's to God," we are to be accountable to man's laws and God's laws — as long as man's laws don't contradict God's laws.

I think you might be surprised at how the two definitions are different. In God's eyes: *"At the heart, accountability is one Christian submitting to the Christ-centered admonition of another Christian in one or more areas of life. Hand in hand with accountability is an attitude of grace and forgiveness, and the taking on of one another's burdens"* (Romans 12:16, Colossians 3:13, Galatians 6:2).[1]

> *"Live in harmony with one another. Do not be proud but be willing to associate with people of low position. Do not be conceited."*
>
> — *Romans 12:16*

> *"Forbearing one another, and forgiving one another, if any man has a quarrel against any: even as Christ forgave you, so also do ye."*
>
> — *Colossians 3:13*

> *"Bear one another burdens, and so fulfill the law of Christ."*
>
> — *Galatians 6:2*

For instance, I recently finished a long fast. I didn't do it alone. I had some friends who were fasting with me. We were "accountable" to each other. That meant we relied on each other as well as God when our strength began to fail. We could call each other and pray, talk, seek God, and "be accountable" to each other over our commitment to our fasts. Being "accountable" to each other and accountable to ourselves felt good! It helped me successfully complete a fantastic fast. I didn't just choose any friends to do the fast with me. I chose friends I knew well and trusted both for their spiritual maturity, their commitment to our fast, and their confidentiality among us. I thought a lot about accountability, and this book, while on my fast. It was a powerful time for me, and I highly suggest a fast if you're so led.

I found this post about accountability from God's point of view, on a biblical leadership site, and it struck a chord with me:

> *"**Accountability is not about what you don't do.** Accountability is not a "confessional" of sorts where we admit things we shouldn't be doing. When we make life about a list of don'ts in order to appear more Christ-like, we not only miss the point, we slide into legalism. Rather, spiritual growth is first a desire to be more like Jesus, to live the life of Jesus, to open our eyes and hearts to the things of God. Cutting out negative behaviors, then, is a **byproduct of a vital relationship with Christ, rather than the central goal.** The parables of Jesus often focused not on the bad that we do, but the good that we left undone. Did you stop for the traveler in need on the side of the road? Did you visit the person you know in prison? Did you clothe someone who needed a coat? Life transformation occurs most by when we start serving rather than our attempts to stop sinning."*[2]

So, God's accountability isn't meant to shame us and blame us. His demand for accountability is mostly a constant reminder that we need His grace daily to live for Him. Christian accountability isn't legalism or "obeying the law." Real accountability is about growing to be more like Christ, not punishing ourselves for our failures.

While we will all ultimately be held accountable to God for our thoughts, deeds, and actions, please keep in mind it's not out of a desire to hurt, shame, or embarrass us. God wants our best. He wants us to be more like Christ, and ultimately, the beings He created us to be. As with all His testing and discipline, accountability is how God stretches us and helps us grow to be more like Christ.

God talks a lot about accountability throughout both the Old and New Testaments. If you haven't memorized James 4:17, now is a good time to do so.

> *"If anyone, then, knows the good they ought to do and doesn't do it, it is sin for them."*

I don't think God could be any clearer. James says that if you know what is right to do, especially in God's eyes, and don't do it, it is sin. This means that if God were to tell you to forgive someone and you say no, you have rejected God and what He represents in your life. You're rejecting the very character of who Christ is.

Jesus talked about accountability in Matthew 12:36: *"But I tell you that everyone will have to give account on the Day of Judgment for every empty word they have spoken."*

Jesus isn't just looking at our actions, but at our words and how we control our tongues. Being accountable with our tongues and words is something we ought to soberly and seriously consider. A simple word can make or break someone. And, on the Day of Judgment, God will remind us of these words, show us the impact they had on others, and express His happiness or displeasure with us. If you can imagine that God is hearing, saving, and weighing every word, be it a joke, a criticism, an encouragement, or a blessing to those around us. He takes everything we say, think, do, or believe in very seriously. He is not impressed by outward appearances or the things we human beings are impressed by. God knows our hearts.

Consider 1 Samuel 16:7, *"But the Lord said to Samuel, "Do not consider his appearance or his height, for I have rejected him. The Lord does not look at the things people look at. People look at the outward appearance, but the Lord looks at the heart."*

Samuel was a mighty prophet, but God had to tell him that while man looks at what a person is on the outside, the Lord concentrates most on the heart inside. God knows our hearts reveal our true intentions. He knows whether we understand and accept what accountability means. He knows if we are capable of committing to doing what is asked of us. And more importantly, He knows if we're ready, mature enough, and responsible enough to be accountable. Are you?

Being accountable means making unpopular decisions. If you've let it be known you're accountable to God, expect others to watch and test you — especially non-believers and Satan. Nothing is as satisfying to the devil as watching an earnest Christian fail, run, or hide from accountability. I imagine the serpent who tricked Eve into tasting the fruit of the tree may have been nearby, laughing at the couple's conversation with God, until he realized God was holding him accountable as well.

Satan wants us accountable and beholden to no one. God wants us accountable to Him so He can protect us, advise us, and steer us clear of the devil's wiles.

Accountability is not a bad thing. It's another opportunity for us to draw closer to God, to become more like Christ, and to be a better witness to non-believers.

Being accountable to man's laws is something we've done since childhood, to one degree or another. We were first accountable to our parents, then to school, our friends and teachers, society, our employer, and our community and society's laws. We all know what being accountable to others in the world means. Many of us assume that if we "get away with something," and can put the blame or accountability on others, or not get caught or taken to task for our words, deeds or actions, that we're okay. Life can even become a game to see how much we can get away with, and how unaccountable we can be. God sees our lack of accountability to man and holds us accountable anyway. You don't get away with anything in this life. And while man's definition of accountability is more legalistic and punitive, accountability to God is a discipline, a way He prepares us to SOAR in His kingdom.

I hope this takes away some of the panic and fear so many of us feel when we see "accountability" as a negative, punishing slap on the hands — or worse — by God. It's not. It's just one of the many things God uses to bring us closer to Him and to make us more like Christ. Don't fear accountability. Embrace it. Honor it. Rejoice in it because it truly does make us more compassionate, more humble, and more attuned to God.

SOARING FOR THE KINGDOM

ACTION ITEMS

- In your quiet time journal, define and write down what accountability to God and man means to you. Refer to this and read it each morning or whenever you have your quiet time.
- Think about your friends and family. Is there someone you trust, someone who is mature in the Lord and who will keep your confidence? Talk to them about your reading this book and ask them to be your accountability partner to ensure you finish reading this book. Ask them to ask you about what you're learning in your quiet time. Share an insight or something that spoke to you as you were reading or praying. God wants us to not only read His Word but share it as well.
- Using a concordance or study bible or Google, search out three different articles or blog posts on what being accountable to God means to different authors. Read the articles and sum up what you've read in a few sentences or paragraphs as suits you. Put this in your quiet time journal.

Chapter 4

Release Yourself from all Encumbrances

R — Release yourself from bondage, sin, and anything that separates you from God and prevents you from soaring.

You cannot reach the pinnacle if you are carrying weight. "Lay aside every weight and sin" so you can SOAR. Release bad habits, hurts, unforgiveness, anger, and regrets, so you let go of the things holding you down. Get rid of the "cage" built from these things that hold you hostage in your own body and spirit.

Years ago, I watched an episode of "Hoarders." It's a television show about people who have a mental illness that causes them to hoard broken, useless items, animals, and even their earwax and body fluids. The level of hoarding on the show is extreme — sometimes to the point where the person or family cannot use the door to their home but must crawl through a window.

There is no rhyme or reason for their hoarding other than their mental illness. While they often call themselves "collectors," the things they collect have no value. If they, for instance, collect dolls,

SOARING FOR THE KINGDOM

tools, or books, those items will often be water damaged, broken, moldy, or useless, with no value other than what the hoarder imagines them to have.

Hoarders will also collect empty fast food bags, broken appliances, and half-eaten food. Many even collect their urine and feces in bottles or buckets they store around the house. Many hoarders have rooms in their houses so filled with trash and junk they can no longer get into the room, let alone use it for its intended purpose.

Some people can no longer get in their bathroom or kitchen and sleep on piles of trash. It's not unusual for a hoarder to have a house so full of junk and trash that it is piled high to the ceiling, with only a "goat path" through the debris for them to move around. The stench is often unbearable, and in time, the sheer weight and condition of the home's contents break down outer walls, beams, and floors, destroying the home.

How did it get that way? Not overnight. The hoarding begins slowly, bit by bit. There's one item, then another. The piles grow a little bit, then a little bit more. The person tells themselves they're going to "pick it up," or "clean," but they don't. They get used to the piles of clothing, the trash, and the bags and boxes of things growing around them. Eventually, they're so overwhelmed they resign themselves to living in a trash heap. It takes the outside efforts of friends and family to come in, clean out the house, and work with the person to address their mental illness. They are just too overwhelmed to take action on their own behalf. They are so attached to their trash they are unable to let even trash and papers, dead animals, and molding, rotting food be thrown away. They need intervention to release their hoard.

What fascinated me about these hoarders is that for most of them, from the outside, no one could tell they were hoarders. Until things really got out of control, these men and women managed to dress well, stay clean and presentable, and even hold down jobs and relationships without anyone knowing they were a hoarder. For some,

Release Yourself from all Encumbrances

even close family members didn't suspect. For others, the adult children had grown up in clutter and a hoarding household.

The other thing that fascinated me was how strongly attached many of these otherwise intelligent and functioning people were to hold on to their trash. Even when the professional cleaners and family pointed out the items had absolutely no value to anyone, they persisted in their hoarding. It's not so different from you and me — only extreme in its practice.

Think about it. Have you ever held on to empty food containers "just in case you needed to save leftovers?" But if we think about it, we probably haven't touched those containers in years. Yet, we hold onto them, reluctant to throw them away.

"Someday," we tell ourselves, "I may need them and won't have them." How often have you said that when someone asked why you were holding onto something? It may be photos with sentimental value or clothes you no longer fit into but that are still in good shape. You'll never wear them again, but you hold onto them thinking, "I might lose that weight," or "It might come back into style."

If you look in your closet, there are probably outfits, purses, shoes, and even makeup you haven't worn or used in months or years. Men, how often do you use the tools, clothes, sports gear, and other items you have? It's just so hard to get rid of things, right? That's a hoarding mentality, even if it's not a behavior yet. If our belongings are well-organized, and not flowing out of our closets, we're not likely to consider it hoarding. But we're all only a few items away from things becoming clutter and clutter becoming hoarding.

While most hoarders are triggered into hoarding by the death of a family member, or the loss of something important to them, hoarding tendencies, like Satan, is always hiding in the shadows, waiting to destroy our lives if we don't stay on top of the things in our lives and homes.

SOARING FOR THE KINGDOM

Unconfessed and unrepentant sin is a kind of spiritual hoarding. We hang onto a grievance with someone here. Remember an argument we had 20 years ago that the person never apologized for? Or we nurse our anger or feeling offended by someone or something we heard on the news or social media. Like hoarders, we need outside intervention, the help of friends and God, and prayer to release our thoughts, actions, and sins that God finds abominable and wrong.

We hold onto our fantasies of getting even or exacting revenge. After all, they're just "thoughts," right? We'd never act on them. We forget that God said we don't have to act on our thoughts. We have to dwell on them and entertain them in our hearts for them to be in sin. Imagine all those small daily incidents multiplying over weeks, months, and years, and you have a hoarding sin problem. Those little incidents may not seem like much, but they are. They block our access to God, who doesn't see "just a little sin." It's a sin, or it's not. That's why it's important to confess our sins as we are aware of them and not save them up for "when we feel like it," or for a Sunday or some other occasion.

A friend of mine recently explained that a snowflake, all by itself, is nothing to worry about. But when snowflakes begin to accumulate on a tree branch, they soon have enough weight to bring a mighty oak crashing to the ground. It's the same with those "small sins" we don't think about. It's that petty or catty remark you make about someone else, or that lie, "I'm so sorry but I'm busy this weekend," we make up to avoid offending someone whose request we turn down with a "white lie."

We may think nothing of them, but over time, those sins, like snowflakes, accumulate and bring us down. They become footholds or permission for Satan to come in and accuse us or affect us. What I have learned in my years in the Bible is that our spiritual lives and our physical lives are intertwined. One affects the other. Our bodies, for

Release Yourself from all Encumbrances

instance, are not our own. When we accept Jesus, we become a temple for the Holy Spirit who dwells inside us.

> *"Or do you not know that your body is the temple of the Holy Spirit who is in you, whom you have from God, and you are not your own?"*

> — *1 Corinthians 6:19.*

Like the hoarder, we become reluctant to let go of our sins, even though we know they have no value and are harming us, and the body that is God's temple. Intellectually we "know" that we want and need that release from all that holds us back from a relationship with God, yet we often fight releasing those sins, those attitudes, that guilt, or those feelings.

Webster's Dictionary defines release as "to allow or enable to escape from confinement; set free." Whether you can see it or not, if you have unconfessed sin in your life, you are confined and trapped by sin. Whether it's sin, or worry, fear, or loneliness, anger, frustration, or sadness, Jesus can and will set us free if we ask Him first, and then let Him. Yes. I said, "let Him." For all the weight and aggravation those things bring us, it's amazing how much we insist on clinging to them, unwilling to be set free. It's as though the more we gather the negative around us, the more secure we feel.

Most people would rather hold onto negative things, be they events, or things people have said to them. They're comfortable in their sin like a hoarder is comfortable in their hoarding. They prefer to hold on to hurts, rather than give them up. Freedom scares them. Who would they be if they didn't have someone to hold a grudge again, complain about, or resent? What would they talk about? We've gotten so comfortable with our aches, pains, and sins that we mistakenly see them as the life raft that keeps us afloat day-to-day. Just like an addict,

SOARING FOR THE KINGDOM

or a hoarder, we can't imagine life without our addiction, no matter how much we want to be free of it.

Are you familiar with the story about a woman in Luke who was bent over for 18 years? She was unable to look up at the sky or gaze into people's faces. Her entire life consisted of staring at the ground, at people's feet, and only at what was immediately in front of her. Yet, she worshipped God regularly and was in the synagogue when Jesus and His disciples saw her.

> *"And behold, there was a woman who had a spirit of infirmity eighteen years and was bent over and could in no way raise herself up."*
>
> *— Luke 13:11.*

Look carefully at that verse. Luke tells us the woman "had a spirit of infirmity." Her posture wasn't from an injury, or birth defect, or accident, or old age. It was from a "spirit" or "demon." Later, in verse 16, Jesus Himself describes the woman as "bound by Satan" for 18 years. And while many, if most of the people Christ healed, came to Him or asked Him to heal them, she did not. Christ called her to Himself.

> *"When Jesus saw her, he called to her and said, "Woman, you are set free of your infirmity."*
>
> *— Luke 6:12.*

Jesus obviously wanted to make a point to the Jewish leaders with this woman. They were in the synagogue on the Sabbath, surrounded by Jewish worshippers and the doubting Jewish leaders.

Release Yourself from all Encumbrances

"The leader of the synagogue, indignant that Jesus had cured on the Sabbath, said to the crowd in reply, "There are six days when work should be done. Come on those days to be cured, not on the Sabbath day."

— *Luke 13:14.*

How does Christ respond to this chastisement?

"The Lord said to him in reply, "Hypocrites! Does not each one of you on the Sabbath untie his ox or his ass from the manger and lead it out for watering? And ought not this woman, being a daughter of Abraham, whom Satan hath bound, lo, these eighteen years, be loosed from this bond on the Sabbath day?"

Jesus was pointing out to the crowds that the woman, who was not only Jewish, but a "daughter of Abraham," (a highly regarded genealogy by the Jews), was also a devout Jew, one who spent much time in the synagogue praying and worshipping God. Despite her infirmity, she was at the synagogue to worship God and on this day, was "released from bondage."

Jesus pointed out her devotion to God, and said it only made sense she should be "loosed from this bond (Satan) on the Sabbath day."

Not every illness is rooted in the spiritual. I'm pointing out that the Bible is clear that spiritual warfare exists and manifests in the physical. Ephesians 6:12 states, *"For our struggle is not against flesh and blood, but against the rulers, against the authorities, against the powers of this dark world and against the spiritual forces of evil in the heavenly realms."* Evil spirits can sometimes cause physical illness, pain, and deformities. So why did Luke, a physician, make a point of telling his readers this?

Luke was a gentile, writing for Gentiles and Gentile converts. He was a close companion to Paul, and he wrote more of the New Testament than any other writer — even Paul.[1] He makes a point of telling his readers that when Jesus touched this woman, she was healed immediately of her 18-year bondage. In some healings, Jesus first casts out a demon, then heals the person. But Jesus did not cast out a demon or spirit of infirmity with her. The spirit was just released.

Some people have to go through a process to heal and experience a release. Jesus made and put mud in the eyes of the blind man in John 9:1-12. The man then had to travel to the Pool of Siloam and wash the mud out of his eyes to regain his sight. The man's blindness was not a spirit, but a physical deformity God predestined for God's glory.

> *"As he (Jesus) went along, he saw a man blind from birth. His disciples asked him, "Rabbi, who sinned, this man or his parents, that he was born blind?"*
> *"Neither this man nor his parents sinned," said Jesus, "but this happened so that the works of God might be displayed in him. As long as it is day, we must do the works of Him who sent me. Night is coming, when no one can work. While I am in the world, I am the light of the world."*
> *After saying this, he spat on the ground, created mud with his saliva, and put it on the man's eyes. "Go," he told him, "Wash in the Pool of Siloam" (this word means "Sent"). So, the man went and washed, and came home seeing."*
>
> — John 9:1

As you can probably tell by now, we're all healed in different ways for different reasons in different seasons. No one can tell you how, if, or when you'll be healed or the process you'll go through to get the release you crave. Some of us may not be healed on this side of Heaven, no matter how much we pray or fast and pray. Healing depends on God's plan for us. However, He guarantees us release

Release Yourself from all Encumbrances

from sin and the weight and distance sin puts between God and us. He promises to sustain us on our sick beds and give us strength.

> *"The LORD will strengthen him on his bed of illness; You will sustain him on his sickbed."*
>
> — *Psalms 41:3*

I can assure you that whether you're praying for healing or being granted the grace to endure your afflictions, it all begins with releasing the thing that keeps you in bondage — sin:

> *"The evil deeds of the wicked ensnare them;* ***the cords of their sins hold them fast.*** *For lack of discipline, they will die, led astray by their own great folly."*
>
> — *Proverbs 5:22-23.*

Who is a sinner? We all are. *"Jesus said, "Very truly I tell you, everyone who sins is a slave to sin." — John 8:34.*

Sin is "the transgression of God's laws." There are the obvious sins — murder, theft, adultery — but God is just as concerned about personal sins like gossip (which He considers an abomination), telling "white lies," holding a grudge, or not being willing to forgive a brother or sisters. Those "small sins" are just as serious as the big sins. When you gossip or tell falsehoods about another, you are killing them and their reputation. If, as Christ said, "You lust in your heart after a woman," you have committed adultery even if you don't act on that lust.

So how can you release the sins that are holding you captive? Confess them. Let them go. Give them to Jesus. Then repent. Repenting is changing direction and attitude. It's committing to adopting a new way of thinking, acting, and feeling. Release from spiritual bondage is

SOARING FOR THE KINGDOM

letting go of the behaviors, attitudes, actions, and habits that no longer serve you. I can't tell you what those are. That's between you and God. Be prepared to feel some pushback as the devil tries to convince you not to let go of sin. He'll try to help you justify holding onto things. You don't have to go it alone. People will help you if you let them, but it may be emotional.

As I watched friends and family members, along with professional cleaners, come together to clear the hoarder's house, I was struck by how difficult it was for all involved. The family could see freedom, the light at the end of the tunnel, but the hoarder could not — at least not while they were still surrounded by their collections, trash, and piles of broken items. Once the house was clean, painted, and restored, however, they were thrilled and relieved. It was usually a painful and teary process to get to that point. But they did it. Some relapsed of course, but many of the hoarders were able to "get it" and wake up and keep their homes orderly.

You may experience the same thing when letting go of your old life, friends, and habits. You may experience an emotional surge and joy that lasts for a week or two, then sink back into despair and depression as your old patterns reemerge and you return to the way you were.

You may think, "I can't do this." You may genuinely want to release whatever habit or practice you want to let go of but feel powerless to do so. I have a friend who is struggling to give up sugar. She's diabetic and has given up every food that is bad for her. She's lost over 100 pounds, eats right, and exercises, but she tells me she can't kick her sodas, which are full of sugar and very bad for her.

She's very discouraged. Rather than support and encourage her efforts, friends try to guilt her and shame her into giving up the sodas, which only makes her crave them more. Sodas may not seem like a big deal, but as she told me, "My body is God's temple, and I want it

56

Release Yourself from all Encumbrances

to be healthy. I'm just really struggling with exactly how to go about it."

To sit in judgment of a brother or sister who is actively seeking God and working to be obedient is to deny that all Christians struggle with sin. If anyone tells you differently, they're lying, enjoy being judgmental, or haven't read their Bible. We are new creations of God, but our sinful nature is still there and will be as long as we're on Earth. Satan is still there attacking us, condemning us, and trying to get us to sin and turn on God. Until we're with God in Heaven, we will continue to struggle with sin. Some of us will struggle more than others, but we all will struggle.

> *James 3:2: "For we all stumble in many ways. If someone does not stumble in what he says, he is a perfect individual, able to control the entire body as well."*
>
> *Romans 3:10: As it is written, "Not even one person is righteous."*
>
> *Romans 7:24: "What a wretched man I am! Who will rescue me from this dying body?"*
>
> *Romans 7:15-17: I don't really understand myself, for I want to do what is right, but I don't do it. 'Instead, I do what I hate. But if I know that what I am doing is wrong, this shows that I agree that the law is good. So, I am not the one doing wrong; it is sin living in me that does it."*

Do you hear yourself saying, "I struggle, God. I struggle with ungodly thoughts. I want to be more like Christ. I want to do better. I hate my sin. Is there hope for me?" Yes! Brokenness and shame over sin is a sign of a faithful Christian, one convicted by the Holy Spirit. But take heart, the answer lies within you.

I remember reading a horrible news story about several women kidnapped and held captive in a house for years and years. From time

SOARING FOR THE KINGDOM

to time, the man who kidnapped and imprisoned them would leave the house, leaving them alone. For a long time, the women didn't even try to escape. But then, one day, one of the women decided to risk it. She clawed her way out of the cage and got free. She was able to escape, go to the authorities, and have the other women rescued. It struck me that, like us, the lock on her cage was on the inside of the cage. She had been inside that cage (house) for so long she believed she could never break free of it, but something holy stirred inside of her telling her she could do it. She could free herself. And with God's help, she did!

If you are addicted to something, be it sugar or sin, you may believe that you are unable to break free — until you *try*. Know that God is right there, whenever, however, you reach out to Him.

Even though your soul has already been freed from the chains of original sin, you can release your sins by taking them to God and asking for forgiveness. In your repentance. Also, ask for the strength of mind to turn away from these same sins in the future. So how do you start? Begin with baby steps. Trust God. Ask him to *renew your* mind–to release Tell Him you're not able to release the things you cling to that separate you from Him and that you need his help to let go.

Next, identify those things that are keeping you on the ground. Commit to seeking God. Have patience and discipline while you build your faith muscles. Don't give in or give up. Tap into the power of your heart to connect as often as possible to God. Take time daily to connect with God for at least 30 minutes. During this precious time, build the muscles of your faith to achieve both *revival of your heart and renewal of your mind.*

Release Yourself from all Encumbrances

Revive your Heart: verses

The word "revive" comes from Latin. It means "to live again, to receive again a life which has almost expired; to rekindle into a flame the vital spark which was nearly extinguished." For Christians, "revival" typically means *renewal* or *revival* of their dedication to God after a time of forgetting or straying from God and His Word. However, when I speak of revival in this book, I am specifically focused on the revival of our hearts. I want you to experience the Holy Spirit surging in your heart and filling you with Christ's love and a new passion for the gospel.

Renew your Mind: verses

> *"Do not conform to the pattern of this world but be transformed by the renewing of your mind. Then you will be able to test and approve what God's will is — his good, pleasing, and perfect will."*
>
> — *Romans 12:2.*

I did not serve in the military, but I have friends who have. One of the things I've learned from them is that the first thing the military does when you join is send you to boot camp for between 8 and 13 weeks, depending on the service you enlist in. In boot camp, you are "broken down" and rebuilt. Your head is shaved, and you are issued the same kinds of pants, shoes, boots, t-shirts, and uniforms. You all look alike.

The military drill instructors even come in and announce there is no "color" or race in the military. The only color they're interested in is green (for the uniform). You dress alike, act alike, walk alike, and even eat the same food in the same way at the same time. You learn to march and move and work in unison. Your mind is "renewed" to

SOARING FOR THE KINGDOM

follow the rules, culture, and purpose of the military. It is, I'm told, something that remains with most men and women for life.

The military's goal is to transform the soldier, seaman's, or Marine's mind to ensure that everyone is "on the same page" when it comes to character, rules, actions, and thoughts. They want to "renew" or transform the mind of their recruits so they all are focused on the same mission and goals.

When we become Christians, we literally become new creatures, too, both physically and spiritually, in Christ. Our minds are renewed, and we begin to focus on our true home — Heaven— not Earth. We learn what God expects, demands, and requires of us. We change the way we think, act, and function. We are "in the world" but "not of the world." It's quite a transformation. Not everyone appreciates who we are or the transformation in our thinking and what motivates us when we decide to follow Christ. Some try to "straddle the fence" and be both world citizens and Christians. But Christ reminds us we cannot serve two masters.

> **"No man can** serve two masters: for either he will hate the one and love the other; or else he will hold to the one, and despise the other, Ye cannot serve God and mammon (money or riches)."
>
> — *Matthew* 6:24.

Release Yourself from all Encumbrances

ACTION ITEMS

- **Identify the sins, the habits, the addictions (be it shopping, binge-watching Netflix, smoking, alcohol or drugs, food, porn, gossip, or whatever keeps you from living for God, and confess them to God.** Write down your sins large and small. Look at them and own them. Confess them to God and thank Him for forgiving you. Ask Him to release you from their grip. Do this every day during your quiet time and as you begin to notice you've sinned. Confess your sin immediately. Keep a "short account" of your sins with God. Don't let the sun set on your anger, sin, or frustration. God wants to hear it all and is ready to listen and help you, but first, you must release your sins.

- **Imagine life without the sins that hold you down.** Spend 10-15 minutes a day imagining life spent closer to God and without the things that keep you from going to Him with your concerns.

- **Praise God for answering your prayers.** God knows what we need before we do. He's answering our prayers before we pray. Time doesn't matter to Him, but it does matter to us. I don't think the woman in the synagogue imagined in her wildest dreams that God would heal her that day. She simply continued to do as she had always done, attend synagogue, praise God, and thank Him for healing. God answered her prayers in a way she didn't imagine, and He will do the same for you. Thank God for releasing you and setting you free from anything and anyone that holds you back.

Chapter 5

The Six Aspects of Living: An Overview of the Basic Structure of All Human Beings

Can healthy living be reduced to six basic aspects? Yes. They are:

- Emotional balance (Heart — the authority or seat of our thoughts)
- Physical balance (Strength)
- Spiritual balance (Soul — Mind, Will, and Emotions)
- Social balance (Man — Luke 2:52)
- Psychological balance (Luke 2:52)
- Purpose (I Corinthians 7:17)

"And Jesus grew in wisdom and stature, and in favor with God and man," (Luke 2:52).

Let's look more closely at this verse. "Jesus grew in wisdom (mind, intellect)." He grew in stature (physical), and He grew in favor with God (spiritual) and man (social)." Does the absence of the term "emotions" mean Jesus had no emotions? Hardly. From His anger and chasing the moneylenders and merchants out of the temple, His tears at Lazarus's death, His compassion and frustration with His

The Six Aspects of Living: An Overview of the Basic Structure of All Hu...

disciples, and His sadness and joy at their actions, Christ certainly displayed emotions. He felt and expressed His emotions regularly throughout His ministry and commented on the disciples when they expressed theirs. The difference between Jesus and most of us is that He was emotionally balanced. And His emotional balance is a lesson and character we are to follow if we are to become more like Christ.

I believe if we are out of balance in any one of the six spheres above, our emotional balance suffers. Rebalancing these structures rebalances the emotions as well as our overall structure.

There are six aspects of living, yet out of all of them, I believe the most critical is the emotional, which consists of the heart, the authority of our body, and the seat of our thoughts. It is the heart that God speaks most about, and what I choose to focus on most. Not only is the heart an amazing organ, with four chambers, pumping blood to and from all our organs, but it is a critical part of our circulatory system — our blood flow. But we have another heart, a spiritual heart, the heart that matters most to God. So important is this, that Solomon tells us to guard our (spiritual) hearts.

> *"Above all else, guard your heart, for everything you do flows from it."*
>
> — *Proverbs 4:23.*

But even the disciples had trouble understanding there was a physical heart and a spiritual heart. They asked Christ to explain the parable that said people weren't defiled by what they ate. After all, Jewish dietary laws were very strict and specific. So, when Jesus called the crowds to Him and said, *"Listen and understand. What goes into someone's mouth does not defile them, but what comes out of their mouth, is what defiles them. Anything you eat passes through the stomach and then goes into the sewer. But the words you speak come from the heart — that's what defiles you. For from the heart come evil*

SOARING FOR THE KINGDOM

thoughts, murder, adultery, all sexual immorality, theft, lying, and slander. These are what defile you. Eating with unwashed hands will never defile you." — Matthew 15:18-20.

He was very clear there were two hearts, both with different roles and both with critical aspects of the Kingdom of God. Understanding these aspects is critical if you want to follow the six aspects of living and the basic structure of all human beings. We are created in the image of God, so we too, are triune beings — having a body, soul, and spirit. Jesus wanted His followers to understand that because God intended blood to represent His ultimate sacrifice — His son and the cross. The Jewish feast days, laws, and practices were not created as laws only. They were to demonstrate and illustrate what was to come — God's redemption of mankind through Christ's sacrifice and death on the cross.

"The life of every creature is in its blood," (*Leviticus 17:14*). Christ tells us. What is in the blood then? It's oxygen, nutrients, and our immune system. Our lives are contained in our blood which is circulated by the heart. While ancient Israel may not have seen all that blood carries and does as we can today, they knew that blood was not only a metaphor for life, but it was life itself. When blood was shed in the Scripture, life usually ended. To remove the blood from someone or something was to remove its life or kill it. Blood is life and sustains life.

The blood of a sacrifice was never to be eaten or consumed. It belonged to God and was given to God on the altar, a foreshadowing of Christ's blood on the cross for us.

"For the life of a creature is in the blood, and I have given it to you to make atonement for yourselves on the altar; it is the blood that makes atonement for one's life"(*Leviticus 17:11*). Atonement for sin was achieved by sacrificing an animal's life in substitution for one's own life until Christ died — and gave us eternal life through His blood and sacrifice.

The Six Aspects of Living: An Overview of the Basic Structure of All Hu...

For all the miraculous and wonderful things our physical and spiritual hearts give us, they are also not to be trusted. Even Jesus never trusted man's heart because He knew they were deceitful and evil —even His own disciples.

> *"The heart is deceitful above all things, and desperately wicked; who can know it? I, the Lord, search the heart."*
>
> *— Jeremiah 17:9-10a*

> Jesus knew this about the human heart; therefore, He didn't commit Himself to anyone because He knew what was in man's heart. Jesus said, *"For from within, out of the heart of men, proceed evil thoughts, adulteries, fornications, murders, thefts, covetousness, wickedness, deceit, lewdness, an evil eye, blasphemy, pride, foolishness. All these evil things come from within and defile a man."*
>
> *— Mark 7:21-23 NKJV*

"Create in me a clean heart, O God, and renew a steadfast spirit within me" (*Psalm 51:10*), should be our prayer to God when we go to Him in worship and praise and ask Him to move in our lives.

EMOTIONAL BALANCE

God is an emotional being. He is described using emotional terms as being loving, generous, patient, slow to anger, and compassionate. But God can be moved to wrath and anger, too. We see it throughout both the Old and New Testaments. Jesus too showed a range of emotions — from His weeping at the death of Lazarus, to His anger and His driving the moneylenders and merchants out of the Temple. We are made in God's image and God has created in us the same emotions He has. Unlike God or Christ, our emotions are rarely as balanced, wise, or purposeful as God's. Our goal, however, is to become more like Christ, and that includes an emotionally balanced life. So, what is the emotional balance? According to a wonderful chapter I read in the book, *One Second Ahead* ...

"Emotional balance is **a state of being aware of our emotions enough to manage them in a way** that is gentle, honest, and wise. Emotional balance comes from having emotional intelligence combined with a trained mind that's able to notice and respond to emotions when they arise."[1]

Throughout the Old and New Testaments, we see the disciples, prophets, King David, Moses, and others talking about, expressing, and acting on their emotions. God gave us emotions so we could understand ourselves and our motivations better, but emotions are not our goal. Balance of them is.

And while emotions and feelings can be wonderful things, they are not to be trusted. We are not to replace the facts of God's Words — the Scripture — with how we "feel" about something, no matter how powerful, inspired, or "good" those feelings may be. When discipling others, our goal is to first help a person re-align their heart with God's Word. Once that happens, then our desires, thoughts, attitudes, and behaviors will result in balanced and godly emotions.

PHYSICAL BALANCE

Physical balance means having a body, physical energy, and strength that ensures we're able to work, interact with family and friends, and worship in a healthy way. A foggy brain, constant exhaustion, various illnesses, and fatigue aren't part of a physical balance. Being overweight, addicted to food, not exercising, sleeping all the time, or being constantly sick is not what God intended for us. Some of our physical imbalance is genetic, some are spiritually based, and some relate directly back to how well we take care of ourselves. What are

The Six Aspects of Living: An Overview of the Basic Structure of All Hu...

we prioritizing? I know many women spend a lot of time, money, and energy on buying the right clothes and using the best makeup, shoes, and outfits. They will spend hours getting ready to go to church or out in public. The outside of their temple is gorgeous! They look good, smell good, and are always well-dressed.

But, on the inside, they are sick. They have headaches, bowel issues, fatigue, moodiness and spend a lot of time at their doctor's office with chest pains and other ailments. They are overweight and/or diabetic, some are smokers, and most don't eat healthily. I'm not judging. I'm just saying a physical balance means more than looking good physically. A physical balance means you are physically active, healthy, and taking care of your body by eating right, getting enough sleep, and paying attention to the inner body as well as the outer body. Does God really care about our physical bodies? He does.

> *"Therefore, I urge you, brothers and sisters, in view of God's mercy, to offer your bodies as a living sacrifice, holy and pleasing to God — this is your true and proper worship."*
>
> *— Romans 12:1*

> *"Do you not know that your bodies are temples of the Holy Spirit, who is in you, whom you have received from God? You are not your own; you were bought at a price. Therefore, honor God with your bodies."*
>
> *— 1 Corinthians 6:19-20*

Our bodies are God's temple! The Holy Spirit dwells within us when we accept Christ and start to follow him. Would you invite an honored guest into your home and not bother to pick up dirty laundry, or trash, or make the bed? Yet so many of us keep on living as we did before we accepted Christ, not even thinking about our physical selves. God is not asking us to become models or bodybuilders. He doesn't want us to make idols of our bodies by focusing solely on making them muscular, lean, and perfect. He only asks that we have a physical balance and a healthy body. A tired body, a stressed body, is more susceptible to Satan's temptations, poor decisions, and sin.

If you want healing and balance, begin by getting your body in balance. Learn to eat well and exercise — even a walk around the block every night after dinner is a start. If you smoke, stop smoking. If you drink too much alcohol, stop. If your diet consists mainly of fried or fast food, add a salad and get your meats grilled, not fried. I'm not saying give up all you love. I'm saying be thoughtful about what you put into your body by remembering it's God's temple. Get enough sleep. Stop working so much you can't function well.

SPIRITUAL BALANCE

Spiritual balance, like the other kinds of balance this section talks about, is about having a balanced spiritual life. We're in the world, but not of it — meaning we still need to maintain an awareness of and participate in the life around us. I would love to spend 24 hours a day, seven days a week, buried in God's Word. Nothing comes closer to Heaven for me than being in His Word, studying it, meditating on it, praying about it, and looking for ways to apply it. I'm never happier than when I'm interacting with God. However, I am still a wife, mother, student, daughter, employee, and friend. I need to have a spiritual balance where I can spend time with Jesus and in the Scriptures, yet still maintain my human relationships and responsibilities. We are to "occupy until He comes," and that includes both "praying ceaselessly" and also tending to our lives on a physical level. God expects us to use our time here on Earth wisely in all ways.

The Six Aspects of Living: An Overview of the Basic Structure of All Hu...

Don't forget, until Christ started his ministry at the age of 30. He was a brother, a carpenter, a neighbor, and a Rabbi — a spiritual leader. He attended the synagogue, studied God's Word, interacted with the religious leaders, and "grew in stature with both man and God." He had a strong spiritual balance in his life.

At the age of 30 when His ministry began, Jesus preached, but He also attended dinners, parties, weddings, and gatherings of people from all walks of life. His mission was to preach the gospel, and He did that, but He never neglected people to focus only on the spiritual. His actions were a balance of healing, casting out demons, tending to the children who ran to Him, and talking to people about Heaven and Hell. He was preaching the Gospel and teaching the disciples the things they would need to know to continue His ministry when He was crucified and then ascended into Heaven. He walked from village to village. He didn't fly in a private corporate jet. He was in the world but not of it. He expects us to do the same.

Paul was a tentmaker, the other disciples were fishermen; or, like Luke, a doctor, a tax collector; or had various other jobs. They continued to preach after Christ rose and ascended, but they also worked. They maintained a spiritual balance. You can still work and keep God first but have a balanced spiritual life.

PSYCHOLOGICAL BALANCE

Many Christians believe that psychology, therapy, or any worldly mental health practices are "unbiblical." I don't believe that. God describes "madness" in both the Old and New Testaments. People who are "mad" or "out of their minds" have been with us since the beginning of time — some of them are mentally ill, and some of them are demon-possessed. Many have genetic or hormonal imbalances. Others have been abused or neglected as children, and still, others have PTSD or other issues from trauma, war, or their jobs (police, first responder, doctors, etc.).

SOARING FOR THE KINGDOM

The topic of mental illness is controversial, and many believers claim there is no such thing or that it's all demonic. The Bible supports both a genetic or physical cause for mental illness, as well as a spiritual cause. For this book, I'll define *mental illness* as "any psychological or physical (*i.e.,* Down syndrome) condition that impairs a person's ability to think, feel, process, and appropriately respond to life."

Finding Christian counselors who know, understand, and can apply God's Word to people's mental health, either through Scripture, Bible study, and Biblical principles or practice is Biblical.

I believe that all mental illness has a physical as well as a spiritual element because spiritual sickness (sin, bitterness, unforgiveness, low self-esteem, fear, anxiety, etc.) is often at the root of physical and mental illnesses.

The negative aspects of life, whether others attack us with negativity, or whether we're bullied, poorly parented, or subjected to outside abuse, can lead to the wounding of our souls — making our psychological state one of deep emotional wounding. We can't think, act, or seek God when we're emotionally wounded. We tend to hate or blame God or believe He doesn't hear us or doesn't care about it. Everything we experience, even the kindness of others, is filtered through our poor psychological filter. Nothing — even good things, and people — can get through to us. We tend to overreact to ordinary events. I remember reading about a man who shot and killed another man because the man inadvertently bumped into him on a city street. His anger and perception that he was not being "respected" by a stranger just walking by him were enough to set off a murderous rage.

If you've ever been the target of someone with "road rage" who felt offended or disrespected because you didn't signal a lane change, or you were driving too close to them, or simply passed them on the road, then you understand that some people will fly into a murderous rage over what the rest of us see as normal life actions. Sometimes a casual remark, a tone of voice, pausing too long, or speaking too

The Six Aspects of Living: An Overview of the Basic Structure of All Hu...

quickly can trigger someone's hidden pain and they react as though we spilled hot water on them. These people are often seen as having an undiagnosed mental illness when in reality they're suffering the effects of an unhealed soul.

Have you ever believed a person was thinking or saying negative things about you even though you had no evidence of that? Because of your negative mental state, low self-esteem, or jealousy, you create a "story" about someone you fear or are jealous of or believe unsubstantiated things about, convinced they mean you harm when they don't.

I once heard of a woman, I'll call her Teresa, who was tasked with training a new hire. Things went great until her boss asked her to train the new employee in how to do Teresa's job. The first thing that went through Teresa's mind was, "My boss is going to fire me! I'm too old, and he's hired this young woman to replace me." Satan had a field day throwing fiery darts and doubts about her boss's plans to fire her once she trained this new employee. Even her co-workers warned her that she was probably going to be terminated. That only added to her stress.

Teresa had grown up in a dysfunctional family and had a history of people mistreating her, lying to her, using her, and then discarding her. It seemed, she thought, that the more she did for others, the more likely they were to abuse and discard her eventually.

Teresa struggled with these feelings most of her life. So, when her boss wanted her to train this new employee for Teresa's job all kinds of red flags, alarms, and fears about being "discarded" yet again flew to the forefront. Teresa cried and considered quitting before they could use her and then fire her. But the Holy Spirit moved her to be calm and pray. She prayed and fasted over the weekend and felt very calm and led to stay by Monday when she told her boss she'd be happy to train the new employee.

SOARING FOR THE KINGDOM

Teresa had decided her job and her future were in God's hands. She would train this new hire as if God Himself had entrusted her with the job. She trusted God had a plan for her no matter what happened. So, she poured herself into training the new girl on how to do her job. She went above and beyond teaching her the basic how-to's. She explained how everything she did impacted the company, how to network, who to go to for specific issues, and how to be an ambassador, not just an employee. She was more than a trainer. She was a mentor and coach, doing all she could to ensure the young woman's success in her job.

She did so well with her training and mentoring that within months, the woman was functioning almost as well as Teresa at the most complex aspects of her job. Then one day, Teresa's boss called Teresa into the office. It was the day Teresa dreaded, as she expected to be laid off. What she heard next had never entered her mind.

"Teresa," her manager said, "I am amazed at the training you have given our new hire. I had planned to promote you to supervisor once you finished training her and we had someone who could do your job. However, you have so impressed the managers across the division we're promoting you to the director of training instead. You'll be working with human resources to train all of our new hires. Of course, you'll be trained in each position, and this will involve a significant pay raise."

Teresa was stunned. She had dreamed of being a supervisor and maybe a manager one day, but God's plans were greater. She almost doubled her salary, responsibilities, and reputation overnight by doing her best and not believing her worst and unfounded fears. She went on to train hundreds of employees before retiring. As the director of training, she was able to influence the company's culture surrounding onboarding new hires and supporting them as they learned. Over the next ten years, she saved the company millions by retaining the talent they found. Turnovers were almost non-existent,

The Six Aspects of Living: An Overview of the Basic Structure of All Hu...

and the people Teresa trained remained loyal to the company through good times and bad — all because Teresa was willing to trust God and commit to serving him regardless of her fears.

She could have given in to her fears and allowed the devil to play all kinds of psychological tricks on her, preying off of her fears of abandonment as a child, to other psychological factors, like low self-esteem and insecurity.

Psychological balance is hard to achieve if we are not fully invested in God's Word and promises. Confessing sin and working to trust Him in everything is a challenge that can require professional Christian counseling. Many of us were not raised to set, communicate, and enforce healthy boundaries. If we were abused, raised in a one-parent household, or didn't have appropriate role models growing up, our psychological traits or proper responses might be skewed.

Not all people are mentally ill or psychologically unsteady. While Jesus directly healed people who were considered mentally ill, He also recognized demonic control in others and cast the demons out (*e.g.,* Mark 1:34; Luke 11:14).

Perhaps the most famous of the mentally ill/demon-possessed men Jesus freed was the demoniac of the Gerasenes. The man was living naked in a cemetery. He was out of control, violent, and by today's standards, was mentally ill.

"They came to the other side of the sea, to the country of the Gerasenes. And when Jesus[2] had stepped out of the boat, immediately there met him out of the tombs, a man with an unclean spirit. He lived among the tombs. And no one could bind him anymore, not even with a chain, for he had often been bound with shackles and chains, but he wrenched the chains apart, and he broke the shackles in pieces. No one had the strength to subdue him. Night and day among the tombs and on the mountains, he was always crying out and cutting himself with stones. And when he saw Jesus

SOARING FOR THE KINGDOM

from afar, he ran and fell down before him. And crying out with a loud voice, he said, 'What have you to do with me, Jesus, Son of the Most High God? I adjure you by God, do not torment me.' For he was saying to him, 'Come out of the man, you unclean spirit!' And Jesus asked him, 'What is your name?' He replied, 'My name is Legion, for we are many,'" (Mark 5:1-20).

Jesus knew otherwise. This wasn't a case of psychological imbalance. It was a case of demonic possession. He confronted the demons in the man and then ordered the legion of demons to come out of him. Immediately after they did, the man was "in his right mind," got dressed, and sat calmly with Jesus, begging to be allowed to follow Him.

While not all mental illness is due to demonic involvement, there may be people diagnosed with mental illness today who are experiencing some sort of demonic influence. Those are people who first need deliverance and then need Jesus. Demon possession of non-believers is still very much a real phenomenon. But Christians, who are indwelt by the Holy Spirit, cannot be possessed. Trust me, the Holy Spirit will not share His temple (our bodies) with demons. Born-again believers may be oppressed, tempted, and harassed by demons, but not possessed.

PURPOSE

The typical stereotype of Heaven as a place where we all sit on clouds playing a harp is amusing and also highly inaccurate. The idea that we'll be free to do what we want to do and play all day is also inaccurate. God is a God who will expect us to work and has designed Heaven around us working. Work won't be like it is here on Earth, but remember, Adam and Eve had jobs in the garden before they sinned. Adam named the animals, and they both took care of the garden. *"And the Lord God took the man and put him into the garden*

The Six Aspects of Living: An Overview of the Basic Structure of All Hu...

of Eden to 'dress it and to keep it,'" (Genesis 2:15). Work didn't become hard until after Adam sinned. But God does give each of us a purpose. On Earth, we each have one or more "gifts of the spirit," and interests and talents God uses to bring Him glory and our happiness. Can we expect anything less in Heaven? God did not punish us by making us work. He increased the effort, pain, and demands we'd have to meet as we worked.

The Bible is clear about how God feels about work. Here are some verses that are relevant, but I'm sure you can find others as well:

- *"If any would not work, neither should he eat." — II Thessalonians 3:10*
- *"A slack hand causes poverty, but the hand of the diligent makes rich." — Proverbs 10:4*
- *"Work with your own hands, as we commanded you; that ye may walk honestly toward them that are without (i.e., non-believers), and that ye may have lack of nothing" — I Thessalonians 4:11,12*
- *"Go to the ant, O sluggard; consider her ways, and be wise. Without having any chief, officer, or ruler, she prepares her bread in summer and gathers her food in harvest. How long will you lie there, O sluggard? When will you arise from your sleep? A little sleep, a little slumber, a little folding of the hands to rest, and poverty will come upon you like a robber, and want like an armed man." — Proverbs 6:6-11*
- *"The sluggard will not plow by reason of the cold; therefore, shall he beg in harvest, and have nothing" — Proverbs 20:4*
- *"You shall not oppress a hired worker who is poor and needy, whether he is one of your brothers or one of the sojourners who are in your land within your towns." — Deuteronomy 24:14*
- *"And the Lord God took the man and put him into the Garden of Eden to 'dress it and to keep it.'" — Genesis 2:15*

SOARING FOR THE KINGDOM

- *"Whoever works his land will have plenty of bread, but he who follows worthless pursuits lacks sense." — Proverbs 12:11*
- *"The hand of the diligent will rule, while the slothful will be put to forced labor." — Proverbs 12:24*
- *"The soul of the sluggard craves and gets nothing, while the soul of the diligent is richly supplied." — Proverbs 13:4*
- *"In all toil there is profit, but mere talk tends only to poverty." — Proverbs 14:23*
- *"Slothfulness casts into a deep sleep, and an idle person will suffer hunger." — Proverbs 19:15*

Even Paul and the other disciples worked when they weren't preaching, which God also considered work. *"Do not take along any gold or silver or copper in your belts; take no bag for the journey, or extra tunic, or sandals or a staff; for the worker is worth his keep" — Matthew 10:5-10*

And, although most Christians are familiar with the fact Paul was a tentmaker, many fail to see beyond his tent-making as merely a job. Paul was a witness for Christ when he preached, instructed, made, and sold tents and used his income to benefit the Christian community at large.

There are professions at all levels for those who want to preach the Word outside of a church. God cares only that we are in His will and isn't as concerned about whether we're mopping floors and digging ditches or caring for patients in a hospital setting as we think He is. As long as our purpose is putting God and the gospel first, and we're working to provide for ourselves and our families, I believe we are in God's will, and He will bless whatever job we have.

The disciples were fishermen and tradesmen. One was a tax collector, another a doctor, and another a tentmaker. Simon was a zealot — comparable to a modern-day lobbyist or politician. Each had

The Six Aspects of Living: An Overview of the Basic Structure of All Hu...

a purpose — both to fulfill Christ's great commission and to provide an income for themselves and their families. Jesus was a carpenter longer than he preached. Until He was 30 years old, Jesus made his living with his hands, a rough job without power tools and other implements modern-day carpenters have to work with.

You won't find anything in the Bible telling you what kind of work or job to take. As long as you're working and are following Christ's will, the job you take won't matter as long as it's in keeping with God's Word and glorifies God. Don't take jobs that are illegal or that malign Christ.

Should you be a bartender, for instance? It depends on whether you see it as a chance to minister and witness to others who might never darken the door of a church or otherwise hear the Gospel. One of the upsides to working in certain professions, like tattoo artist, bartender, etc., has a lot to do with your past and your reason for pursuing that job choice. Is a bartender at Applebee's or some other food/bar restaurant different from a bartender at a bar in a "bad" neighborhood? Ask yourself if you're putting yourself in a place where the temptations outweigh the opportunity to witness. Will you witness or be allowed to witness there?

Some Christians say one should never be a professional athlete because sports is "too ego-centered." But I say, "What about Tim Tebow?" He's very much a visible Christian and has no overblown ego. The Fellowship of Christian Athletes is an organization that reaches millions through sports.

"Vocation" comes from the Latin word for "calling." The doctrine of vocation means that God assigns us to a certain life — with its particular talents, tasks, responsibilities, and relationships. He then directs, leads, or calls us to that career, either because of the interests and talents He's given us or plans to give us.

SOARING FOR THE KINGDOM

"Only let each person lead the life that the Lord has assigned to him, and to which God has called him. This is my rule in all the churches." (I Corinthians 7:17). God never calls us to sin.

I believe any career, other than those which are illegal, is a calling from God and is a valid career from which to serve Him. So strictly speaking, there are no unlawful vocations; the question should be whether or not a particular way of making a living is a vocation at all.

Some jobs will give you an opportunity to share Christ through your abilities, others through your contact with people (like sales or customer service). Those are the things you should pray about.

The Six Aspects of Living: An Overview of the Basic Structure of All Hu...

ACTION ITEMS

- List the areas of your life you think could be more balanced. Remember, the six aspects are: psychological, spiritual, physical, emotional, social, and purpose.
- Make a list of one to three things you could do in each area to create more balance in your life.
- Set a goal for achieving balance in one area of your life. Once you've worked on that area for 90 days, add another area, and so on. Again, new habits take 30-45 days to form and 90 days to master them. By forming a new habit in each area, you can get closer to balance in less than a year.

Chapter 6

Aspect Number One: Seek an Emotional Balance

I could hear his screams from halfway across the store. A young child was being denied something he desperately wanted. I don't know if it was a candy bar or a toy or something shiny that caught his eye, but I did recognize that scream from having heard it with my children. It was part frustration, part anger, part panic, and part fear. He wanted what he wanted, and he wanted it now.

I moved closer to the checkout line and saw them, a young boy about two years old and his young mother, calmly looking at magazines while she waited in line. He kept screaming, and she kept shaking her head and softly saying, "No, Justin. You can't have candy."

At some point, her "no" must have registered with him. He could see his screaming wasn't working, and it dawned on him that he wouldn't get what he wanted. His crying slowly began to ebb until he was silently sniffing and hiccuping while his mother stood calmly by. She wasn't angry or impatient, just level and balanced, as if this was another lesson her son needed to learn. She spoke to him calmly, distracting him from the candy he wanted.

Aspect Number One: Seek an Emotional Balance

I was impressed that she was strong enough to let him scream and not give in to his tantrum for fear of looking mean or like a poor parent to other shoppers. On the contrary, several other women in line complimented her on "not giving in." One woman leaned over and laughed and said, "If you give in to them this young, they'll wrap you around their finger when they're teenagers."

It was an impressive display of emotional balance in the face of her child's out-of-control emotions. She was going a long way toward teaching him patience and emotional balance, I thought. The entire scene couldn't have lasted more than a few minutes, although I'm sure it seemed much longer to the boy and maybe even his mother.

How often have you or I felt those same feelings of frustration when we were denied something we really wanted? Maybe it was a job, or recognition, promotion, a trip, or an item we couldn't afford. We didn't fall to the floor and launch into an all-out screaming fit because we've learned that's not appropriate or welcomed by those around us. But we sure felt like doing that. Or, we may have screamed into a pillow, vented to our spouse or a good friend, or just laid down on our bed or couch and had a good cry.

Those are the adult versions of pitching a fit — we find or call up a friend who will let us vent and scream and cry about how "unfair" something or someone was. Then we complain until we're exhausted, or our friend tells us, "Enough already!"

We have the skills to communicate our displeasure better than a toddler or non-verbal baby, but the feelings behind our actions are often as out of balance as the toddler. Outwardly, we look and mostly act like mature adults, but inside, we're feeling the whole gamut of negative, explosive, extreme emotions. For some of us, those emotions are stronger than those of friends and family. We may get so upset we can't function for the rest of the day. We may fume and fuss and snap at everyone around us. Those feelings, and how they unbalance us

SOARING FOR THE KINGDOM

and cause us to focus on the negative or the event, may last hours, days, or even weeks.

We may be angry with a coworker, or our employees, or students, or someone under our management. Or we may feel frustrated with a boss, teacher, or supervisor. There's nothing wrong with feeling upset or even angry. But when our emotions take over and distract us or get us into trouble. it's time to check our emotional balance.

I'm not immune to emotional extremes and imbalance, or even waves of emotions — especially anger. My response is not always what anyone would consider "spiritual" or balanced either! I have some questions I've never really asked before. Questions like, "Father God, I've served You faithfully, I love You with all my heart. I don't understand how something like this could happen." My daughter was attacked recently, and I felt helpless, enraged, confused, and angry.

My daughter was already fragile. She already deals with what is considered a mental illness; her anxiety and depression are not circumstantial. I had anger towards her attacker, I don't know who it is or was, but I could hurt him right now. I'm that angry.

For the first time, I find myself in the position of feeling like my values were destroyed. I went from feeling like I could forgive anyone for anything until I was faced with my child being harmed. I have to ask, "Can I forgive this person?" I'm a mother, there were just all these waves of emotion, and I have to keep them bottled up because our daughter is fragile. Bottling them up makes them even more intense, and volatile — like shaking a bottle of soda before taking the lid off. I feel like I'll explode if I uncap my feelings. If my husband and I allow her to see how we are feeling, it will get inside of her, and probably prevent her from healing.

There's a lot of hurt. There are waves of various emotions, all extreme, and the challenge of making sure I hold back my tears

Aspect Number One: Seek an Emotional Balance

because I have to be strong for her. I thought that losing a loved one to death was the worst feeling you could ever feel, but what we are experiencing right now is the worst thing I've ever felt in my life. I really feel helpless.

Writing about feeling a lack of balance makes my feelings more intense. It's as if God wants me to look at my emotions, which He is because I don't want to look at them. I don't want to journal. I don't want to see or feel what's happening inside me right now.

I'm one of the millions of Christians who look like they're holding it together, but you know inside you're really not. It's the first time I've encountered something that I really can't even put on paper. And writing and journaling have been my outlet for 25 years. But I don't want to put this on paper, because I don't even want to look at it, I don't want to think about it. She's angry; she's angry with God.

She doesn't understand why He didn't prevent it. I can't understand why He allowed it to happen either. As much as I love Him, I hear myself questioning Him. I cannot, in my human state, imagine there is a reason for this attack. Why God? Why? There are millions of believers asking Him the same question about things happening in their lives — "Why God? Why? Why my son or daughter? Why this disease or death now? Why this loss, this injury, this betrayal?"

It dawned on me there are a lot of people walking around that look like they are balanced, but they're not. There's an internal imbalance. That's what mine is. Every day, for the two days I went into the office, no one knew what had happened to my daughter, or how I felt about it, and they would never know based on my presentation of myself. I hid it so well. Most of us do.

On the inside? There's wave after wave after wave of emotion. Sometimes the waves calm down, and I feel like everything is okay. And then there's a wave, and all of a sudden, I think about the perpetrator or the horrific event, and I'll have a wave of negative, sometimes almost vile emotion.

How do non-believers get through these times? I ask myself that because I can't imagine being where I am right now without God. That's the thing about being saved because we don't keep ourselves in balance. He does. God is keeping me in this process; He's keeping us during this process. And He knows that because I'm still in this space of anger and hate towards this person but it doesn't mean that I do not love Him. He knows that. He knows those who are His. Peter denied Him, but he came back and served him wholeheartedly with great passion. He knows this is not going to cause me to walk away from Him. He knows it is not going to cause me to stop serving him.

But has it been a distraction? Yes, definitely. Is it a push, to push through the emotions to continue doing the things that I need to do? Yes. But that's what makes me human. I had to finally tell myself, "You and your family are not exempt from tragedy." Although if anyone had ever told me that we would be facing a tragedy like this, I would never have believed it. Because it's something you just really don't think will come to your doorstep if you trust and believe in God. But He never promised us a painless life.

I believe, as hard as it is to believe sometimes, that my God is a God of purpose. I know He's going to bring a better thing out of this. I know my daughter will be able to minister and share with someone else once she's whole and healed, and I know only because of the grace of God that she's doing as well as she is. I see Him at the same time, but there are times when I just don't understand how we got here with this. Sometimes I'm angry; there are times I want to throw in the towel. I want to scream at God, "Lord, I feel like, for the majority of my life, I have served You. For most of my life, I've done so much for so many other people, why this? Why my daughter?"

There are times I feel like, "After all I've done for you, serving you, loving you, and this is what I get? These are the types of scars you

Aspect Number One: Seek an Emotional Balance

want me to carry?" Yet, If I do not hold onto Him, I will fall apart. Like Peter said, "Lord, to whom shall we go? You have the words of eternal life." We see things in the time they happen. God sees them in eternity.

What happens when we get out of emotional balance? We begin to self-destruct. Some go deeper and darker than others. But all the destructive things that people are doing, they're not doing it just because they find pleasure in it. They are in pain, trying to escape that pain in ways that seem to make sense to them.

Some people do things because, emotionally, they are out of whack. And they are looking for things to cover up or medicate their feelings. They're hoping that the things they are doing, the destructive decisions, and the way they are choosing to put a band-aid on their hurt and their pain will help them to heal, will help them to bring balance. It won't.

A lot of people are dealing with anger, lashing out, and hurting others. As psychologists often say, "Hurting people hurt people." Many people are not dealing with these issues because they just want to, or because they just didn't get their way. A lot of people are covering up. I'm one of them. You would never know if I met you on the street. You would never know what we are dealing with in our home right now. That's a mask. I confess. I'm wearing a mask and acknowledging that it is difficult but important. I want readers to know they're not alone, that it's not easy, but that God is with you every step of the way, whether you're accusing or screaming at Him, sobbing in His arms, or ignoring Him because of the anger. He is God. He is there. He saw this attack before it happened. It's not a random, meaningless crime. He has a plan, and while I don't know what it is, I have to trust Him.

Life doesn't stop after the attack. The world goes on. Commitments go on. It makes it feel surreal. I wanted everything to stop and acknowledge this horrific crime against my daughter, but it didn't.

SOARING FOR THE KINGDOM

Life goes on. I was on my way to speak at a women's conference where I was already scheduled to speak. On my way there, I'm praying to the Lord, I'm saying, "God, I don't know if I can do this ... " and here came a wave of emotions, while I was thinking about my daughter and my pain for her. And my pain is nothing compared to her pain. Waves of emotions, and I'm thinking, "Lord, I really don't know if I can go in here and do this. I don't know if I'm going to get up and forget what I'm supposed to say. Even though I have everything here in front of me, I just don't know if I can keep a clear mind."

And you know what I said? "My emotions are all over the place." I acknowledged that. I didn't try to justify, ignore, or pretend they weren't. That's step one. God can't help us if we aren't honest with ourselves and with Him. He already knows everything about us and what's happening, but He needs us to come to Him with that pain and talk to Him about it. I say," O, Lord, protect my children so that they never hurt again in their life." I don't know if He will answer that prayer with a "yes," a "no," or a "maybe." I have to wait and see.

I wanted Him to know how much I love them. Not that I love them more than Him, but the pain of a mother for her children, when a mother experiences great pain, and there is no greater pain than what your children are going through. You will do anything for them.

I believe there are a lot of people who are hurting. They just really want the pain to stop, and they're willing to do anything. They're willing to sit down on their purpose, on their calling — whatever it is. They're willing to do whatever it would take to stop the pain and regain balance. And then I asked myself, "Suppose I stop, and then everything just changes instantly? And I missed out on this opportunity because I decided not to trust You wholeheartedly?" It's a wave of emotions. I go back and forth — playing volleyball with God, emotional volleyball. Back and forth and back and forth.

Aspect Number One: Seek an Emotional Balance

There's the saying, "Time heals all wounds," but I believe you can give a wound time, but without medicine or God's divine intervention, no, it won't heal. But when you combine medicine and time, that's the formula for healing. In this case, the medicine is God — getting closer to Him in my pain, in my confusion, in my anger, and in my thoughts and feelings. If you've experienced the loss of a child or had anything happen to your children, you know the depth of the pain you feel for them. You can't just check out and walk away.

"Yeah, though I walk through the valley of death, I will fear no evil. God is with me." And He is. He truly is.

So, this year my daughter was attacked. I lost my brother, suddenly, and unexpectedly. I have also had more extreme things happen to me than I could have imagined were possible. I'm not complaining or asking for sympathy, but I want to emphasize again that no matter how close our walk with God or how well and how close we stay in communion and communication with Him, we are **not** guaranteed a painless life.

The disciples were beaten, shipwrecked, jailed, abused, stoned, and crucified. Following Jesus is not an easy path and never has been. God didn't say it would be. So why all these events and challenges and pain and emotional unbalance? God is building my faith, your faith, and our faith. If you think that's unfair, think for a moment. How do we build muscles? We tear them down, rip apart the fibers, experience the pain and soreness, and then over time, watch our muscles grow. That's how muscles are built — through pain. We are made stronger through adversity because we rely more on God when things are going badly. When things are going well and we have "enough money," a good job, and easy life, we're much less likely to turn to God for His help. We think, "I've got this." We don't. Satan is still out and about, walking up and down the world to find people to destroy.

SOARING FOR THE KINGDOM

God is working in us to prepare us for Kingdom Life, not this life. And that includes the balance in all aspects of our life. It means learning to be in control of, and aware of our emotional states. I'm not saying you can control your rage or pray away your grieving. I'm saying God doesn't take those things away, but He does equip us with the peace and faith to get through whatever comes at us. Different people respond to adversity and anything else with their own methods. That's fine. You do you, as they say, and find what works to keep you in the Word and walking with God.

My two favorite ways of achieving or restoring emotional balance are fasting and journaling. Yes, I do get out of balance, too. There's nothing wrong with failing or falling or getting out of balance unless we don't get back up and get in the "fight." Fasting and journaling are how I get back on my feet —doing what brings me closer to God. The more time I'm in the Word, or fasting and praying or journaling about my experience, the more faith I have in God to do what His will is in the situation.

When we ask God for "patience," He doesn't just give us patience. He gives us lives filled with things that teach us patience — like traffic, long lines, whiny, screaming children, or infuriating bosses. He places us in situations where we learn to develop patience. If your child wants to learn financial responsibility, how do you teach them? You either encourage them to get a job and then work with them to teach them what to do with their money, or you give them an allowance from which they learn to pay their own expenses. When the money runs out, and it will, it's up to them to figure out how to make more or stretch their resources. Suffering brings pain, but it brings faith too.

> "We are troubled on every side, yet not distressed; we are
> perplexed, but not in despair; persecuted, but not forsaken;
> cast down, but not destroyed; always bearing about in the

Aspect Number One: Seek an Emotional Balance

body the dying of the Lord Jesus, that the life also of Jesus
might be made manifest in our body ... So then death
worketh in us, but life in you ... For which cause we faint
not; but though our outward man perishes, yet the inward
man is renewed day by day."

— II Corinthians 4:8, 10, 12, 16

Whether we like it or not, pain is part of learning. The toddler I mentioned at the beginning of this chapter felt real pain, emotional and psychological pain. But he didn't experience harm. When I go to the doctor, or the dentist, or have a child, I experience pain. But that pain doesn't harm or kill me. There's a difference. There is pain that is part of healing, and pain that is part of destroying. I often reflect on what Paul and the disciples went through in terms of pain. Paul, for instance, told the Corinthians:

"Of the Jews five times I received forty stripes save one. Thrice
was I beaten with rods, once was I stoned, thrice I suffered
shipwreck, a night and a day I have been in the deep; in
journeyings often, in perils of waters, in perils of robbers,
in perils by mine own countrymen, in perils by the
heathen, in perils in the city, in perils in the wilderness, in
perils in the sea, in perils among false brethren; in
weariness and painfulness, in watchings often, in hunger
and thirst, in fastings often, in cold and nakedness. Beside
those things that are without, that which cometh upon me
daily, the care of all the churches."

— 2 Cor. 11:24-28

Would you trade your current challenges and pain for Paul's? He wrote this, by the way, when he was in prison, shackled, bound, cold

SOARING FOR THE KINGDOM

and hungry, and most likely beaten by his guards. Would you take 39 lashes not once, but five times? Would you survive a shipwreck and being in the ocean for two days? What about robbers and betrayals by friends? How would you cope with nakedness and cold? We think we have problems, but I'm guessing none of us would gladly trade them for what Paul or any of the disciples endured.

The depth and length of pain depend on us and how we respond to it. Do we trust God and have faith He is acting on our behalf? Remember, Job had boils over his body for more than a year and yet never cursed God. His devotion and faith in God were incredible. I believe God doesn't give us more than our faith or our relationship can handle. He may push us right to the edge, and He'll often do it after we've been on a mountaintop for some time. My recent fast put me on a mountaintop where I was closer to God than before. Now I'm dealing with my daughter, work, school, writing, and so much more. I do what I always do when stressed, under attack, or feeling overwhelmed with what's happening:

1. I find a quiet and serene place for personal time in prayer.
2. I constantly tell myself in times of sorrow that it could always be worse, that nothing lasts forever, and that there is an end to all things. I ask God to give me the strength to endure to the end.
3. In sorrow, I worship! This helps me take my focus off my problem and maintain my focus on the Who that can get me through the pain and resolve the situation.
4. In both sorrow and happiness, I praise God! Praise warms my heart and reminds me of God's goodness in prior good and negative situations.
5. I find a scripture that pertains to the area of pain, and I read it, say it out loud and reread it, say it out loud and reread it and say it out loud until it saturates my heart and refuels my faith.

Aspect Number One: Seek an Emotional Balance

6. You have to create a personal path with the Word, Worship and Prayer to stay on course and help you find your way back when life causes you to derail.

Like the parent denying her child a treat he wanted, we may be the person who has to make decisions that may lead to others feeling angry, upset, or frustrated even though our decisions are the best things for them in the long run. No matter who we are, or where God has planted us, emotional balance can be an ongoing struggle until we learn the secret to finding balance — resting in God.

In the book, *One Second Ahead,* by Rasmus Hougaard, there's a chapter on emotional balance that sums up very succinctly what emotional balance is:

*"Emotional balance is **a state of being aware of our emotions enough to manage them in a way** that is gentle, honest, and wise. Emotional balance comes from having emotional intelligence combined with a trained mind that's able to notice and respond to emotions when they arise."*[1]

The key here is "a state of being aware of our emotions enough to manage them." God made us to have emotions and to feel them strongly and appropriately. The strength of the emotion isn't what makes us emotionally imbalanced. Any emotion, positive or negative, can intensify to the point where we lose control. Think of young children overwhelmed with positive emotions like Christmas, or a birthday party, a favorite relative visiting, or too much sugar! Emotions aren't bad. It's whether we can manage them appropriately that matters.

Depression, anger, grief, and hopelessness can be deadly when they throw us off balance. We're more likely to make poor or downright bad decisions when we're feeling unbalanced. That's why experts advise people not to make any significant decisions, like buying or selling a house or other property, getting remarried within a year of a

SOARING FOR THE KINGDOM

divorce, moving cross-country, or dating after a breakup. When our emotions are that powerful, we tend to be unbalanced, and more likely to make poor decisions as a result.

God wants us to have emotions, but He doesn't want our emotions to go beyond what we can control. And, when they do, He tells us what to do with them to bring them back into control. Prayer, reading the Scriptures, meditating on His Word, and learning how people throughout the Bible managed their emotions — or didn't — and the consequences. For instance, in Numbers 20, God told Moses to speak to the rock in the desert to bring forth water for Israel:

> *Num. 20:8 — "Take the rod; and you and your brother Aaron assemble the congregation and speak to the rock before their eyes, that it may yield its water. You shall thus bring forth water for them out of the rock and let the congregation and their beasts drink."*

Frustrated with God's people, and who wouldn't be! Moses chose to strike the rock instead of speaking to it. God punished Moses for being disobedient. Moses was disobedient because he allowed his frustration to emotionally unbalance him.

> *"So Moses took the rod from before the Lord, just as He had commanded him; and Moses and Aaron gathered the assembly before the rock. And he said to them, "Listen now, you rebels; shall we bring forth water for you out of this rock?" Then Moses lifted up his hand and struck the rock twice with his rod; and water came forth abundantly, and the congregation and their beasts drank."* (*Num. 20:9-11*)

Earlier in Exodus, God did instruct Moses to strike the rock to produce water:

Aspect Number One: Seek an Emotional Balance

Ex. 17:6 — "Behold, I will stand before you there on the rock at Horeb; and you shall strike the rock, and water will come out of it, that the people may drink." And Moses did so in the sight of the elders of Israel.

As a result of his disobedience, God forbade Moses to enter the promised land. It wasn't just his disobedience God was punishing. God wanted to ensure that the Hebrews understood the significance of the "rock," which was Christ being sacrificed once for our sins. It was a hard lesson to learn, and the consequences must have been devastating for Moses.

What often appears to be "no big deal" when we become emotionally unbalanced can lead to words, anger, accusations, and actions that can lead to great consequences. When we act in the moment of uncontrolled emotions, be it anger, frustration, vengeance, or even lust, or excitement (telling a secret we've been asked to hold in confidence, for instance), we rarely weigh the consequences.

A mature Christian will stop and consider the consequences of their emotional state. They're aware of what they're feeling and thinking and can step on the brakes and look at what could happen if they act inappropriately because of their emotions. That's emotional balance. The young mother, I'm sure, felt anger, shame, frustration, and embarrassment. After all, her child was making shopping an unpleasant experience for everyone within earshot of his screams.

Yet, she resisted shaming, humiliating, or punishing the child for his emotions. She was able to see the big picture; that by training him, he wouldn't always get his way, or get what he wanted, was what he could expect to experience in his family. What mattered at that moment was not what others thought, but what her son's character would be in the future if she gave in to his demands. She made an emotionally balanced choice, even though it wasn't easy. Someone had obviously trained her in how to do this.

SOARING FOR THE KINGDOM

We are not born emotionally balanced. That's why until they're trained and disciplined to become aware of and control their emotions, young children cry, pitch fits, and scream to get their way. They are only aware that they're feeling something they don't want to feel. Crying, screaming, and pitching a fit is their only outlet. Give them enough timeouts and teach them that screaming is not acceptable behavior, and they will soon learn to control those feelings and substitute their actions with words instead.

As I considered all this while standing in the checkout line for a few minutes. I looked over at the child. He was crying, his eyes were all red and swollen, and his face was puffy. But he was not screaming. His mother was holding his hand, not embarrassed, not angry, just calm. Every now and then she would bend over and hug the boy, or kiss his cheek, say something in his ear, and smile. By the time I got up to the clerk, the boy was laughing and seemed fine. He didn't have a toy or treat in his hand, and from what I could tell, he had learned that his behavior was not acceptable. He was still loved, and he seemed to know that, but he was one step closer to bringing his emotions under control.

It wasn't at that same visit, but another where I saw and heard a 10-year-old boy curse his mother and even slap her when she told him "no." I shudder to think of what that parent faces when the child is 14, 16, or a grown adult. Society and many police officers throughout his life will have to be the ones who step in and disciplines this boy. They will learn about emotional balance the hard way — through jail and legal action or by another emotionally unbalanced person beating them during an encounter where neither party can control themselves.

Look around. People do well to hide their pain and feelings. But if you pay attention, you can see others struggling emotionally, too. You're not alone. Others are going through cancer and treatment,

Aspect Number One: Seek an Emotional Balance

losing a child to war, suicide, disease, or drugs. They are struggling in their marriages. Some couples have just filed for divorce, or one spouse has caught another cheating. Some have lost friends to Covid-19, and others to heart attacks or strokes. Some never got a chance to say goodbye, or "I'm sorry," or "I love you." We are all in pain.

In a way, not sharing the details with others forces us to turn to God instead. He's always there, always listening, always caring, and always offering His peace, a peace which "passes all understanding." I cannot explain the peace that comes over me when I pray and relect on His Word. I still see and feel the pain, but I'm comforted and reassured in the midst of it, that God is in control.

As a child, did you ever scrape your knee and have your mother hug you, maybe pick you up, then wash your scrape and put a Band-Aid on it? It still hurt, but her presence, her love, her caring, her touch, her kiss on your head or cheek, and her reassurance that you were "going to be okay" overwhelmed and diminished the pain of the scrape. You were aware of it but focused on the love coming from your mother. If you didn't have that experience, I'm sorry. It's one of my favorite memories of my childhood — knowing and experiencing parents who were there for me.

Even if you have never experienced that kind of compassion and care from humans, please know it's there from God if you open yourself up to it. When we become emotionally unbalanced and our world starts turning, and we start crying out in anger and frustration, fear, and confusion. God is there. He sees it all and is ready to come to our side and love us if we ask Him.

Feeling emotionally fragile or unbalanced is a lifelong struggle, but it gets easier the more we learn to get our emotions under control and in balance. Have you ever had a bad day — one where traffic cuts you off, strangers are rude, friends and family are critical, and nothing you do turns out right? You may snap at people you love or yell at those

SOARING FOR THE KINGDOM

who are only trying to help you. Emotional balance is not a "learn it, set it, and forget it" kind of skill. It's more like balancing on a giant rolling ball, stepping forward, then back, then side-to-side, trying to find our center of balance, if only for a moment. Yet, the more we practice balancing, the better we get at it.

Aspect Number One: Seek an Emotional Balance

ACTION ITEMS

- **Conduct an emotional assessment of your life over the past month.** Think about the times you felt stressed, angry, moody, frustrated, or sad over the past month or the past week if that's all you can remember. Write down as much as you can about your emotional swings, good or bad, what your general moods were, and what caused them. This will give you a baseline to start becoming more aware of your emotions and your triggers. Be honest. Write down anything that comes to mind. You won't be sharing the paper with anyone but yourself and God. And He already knows you better than you know yourself, so don't stress over that.

- **Spend the next week, or preferably the next month, being aware of your emotions and writing them down as they happen.** You don't have to write a lot. You can simply write down your most dominant emotions and make a check under them when you feel them. Include a time of day, and a line about what triggered the emotion. Your journal entry might read,

  ○ "7:55 a.m., frustrated, angry. The children were not ready for school and missed the bus. I was late to work because I had to drive them to school."

  ○ 10 a.m., frustrated and angry, disappointed. Employee failed to have the report I requested finalized for an important meeting.

  ○ 5:45 p.m., tired, angry, and disappointed. Husband failed to start dinner as he promised, and the family ended up eating cereal and junk food for dinner. I was looking forward to a hot meal.

- **Create a strategy to help you balance your emotions.** Learning to balance our emotions doesn't happen

SOARING FOR THE KINGDOM

overnight. Some people can bring their emotions back into check by simply becoming more mindful and aware of them by following the exercises above. Some people need a therapist or other psychological professional to help them develop the skills and tools they'll need to balance their emotions. Prayer, a Bible study around emotional balance, and journaling are all ways to begin to get your emotions under control. Breathing exercises, walking, exercising, listening to music, determining what things and people upset you most, and avoiding them, can help you balance your emotions.

Chapter 7

Aspect Number Two: Seek A Physical Balance

Being in college puts me around more young people than other adults my age. And young people these days tend to be either in better shape than I was in my 20s, or much worse shape than I've ever been. I'm not judging, I'm noticing. We live in a culture where physical balance and looks (for example a fit and toned body, and facial beauty), are important. Clothes, makeup, how we look, and how we come across to others, are the superficial balance many assume equates with a "physical balance." But our physical balance is so much more.

A healthy physical balance means eating right, exercising, praying, being active, and taking care of our bodies. That means being aware of our physical selves. There's nothing wrong with being fit, toned, and active unless the gym and working out becomes the temple where you worship your body instead of the God who created your body.

I'm not really a gym person. I don't lift weights. There's nothing wrong with weights or the gym, but I like to run. I used to jog 10 miles once a week, every Saturday. While I lived in Indiana, I ran with two other friends. We jogged 10 miles together every Saturday morning. We'd jog at 5 a.m. while it was still dark. That's my set time for everything — for prayer, exercise, and getting my day started. I usually start my day at 4:30 or 5 a.m.

So, every Saturday at 5 a.m., we were out jogging on a trail, and we just stumbled onto the 10 miles. We didn't know we were doing 10 miles. We would start at 3 miles, at least. Once you start jogging, you get what's called a "runner's high" and the adrenaline starts going and you feel great. You don't want to stop. One day all three of us were like, "Hey, we don't want to stop. Let's keep going." So, we did.

One day after maybe a year, we decided to calculate the distance and that's how we found out that it was 10 miles. So, it was 5 miles. Let me be clear. We would jog 5 miles up and walk 5 miles back. On Saturdays, we did a total of 5 miles of jogging, and 5 miles of walking. That was on Saturday. We took Sunday and Monday off. So Tuesday through Friday, we did 2.5 miles at 5 a.m. And that was the best time of my life, it was a remarkable time. Fast forward – we relocated to Ohio, and I couldn't find anyone with that level of commitment. My husband didn't feel comfortable with me going out by myself at 5 am, and he wasn't willing to go with me. So, I had to put that to the side.

Then I started going to our local community recreation center. It's a nice center. It has an indoor track. You have to do 10 laps to get one mile and it was too cumbersome ... circle after circle, and I just could not do that. I'm an outdoor runner. I like to run outdoors or walk outdoors. I don't like to do anything indoors at all.

People ask me, "If you don't run now, are you out of physical balance?" First of all, how much or how often you do something isn't considered being in or out of balance unless you do nothing or too much. If you don't do any kind of physical activity, even just walking or cleaning, or playing a game of basketball with friends, then you're out of balance because you're not doing anything. But if you do too much, to the point where it interferes with your life, or your family, or

Aspect Number Two: Seek A Physical Balance

your work or school obligations, it's too much. Do you see the difference?

It's not the amount of physical activity you do, but whether that amount is in balance with the rest of your life. I used to run 10 miles a day, but I don't do that now. That doesn't mean my life is out of physical balance. It just means my routine has changed, and with it, the amount of time I run. Life happens to us all, and as long as we adjust to accommodate those changes while still getting in the physical, mental, emotional, social, financial, and spiritual things we need to do to stay balanced, we're fine.

You may find that what you can do and have time to do, changes with each season of your life. As a college student or young person, you may have more time and opportunities to travel, exercise and work out, or date. Once you're married and if you have children, work, your family, and your spouse will require more time, and your daily runs, or spending hours playing golf, or at the gym, or doing the things you love will require cutting back. You're doing them less but doing them is still a part of the balance you need to be healthy, to grow, and to be responsible to those you love.

I can always identify whether I'm in or out of balance with an image of a scale. I can always tell when I'm tipping the scale to one side more than the other side. If the scale is way down on one side than on the other side, I identify where the imbalance is. Am I spending too much time at work? Or am I on social media more than I should be meaning I'm neglecting my family and not paying attention to them? I look at all six aspects of life and I tweak those and get everything back in balance. It's not something you can do the first time you try. It's taken me years to recognize when part of my life is out of balance. The more you focus and are aware of each area of your life, the easier it will get. It will become a lifestyle, a habit, and not something you feel like you have to do each day or each week.

SOARING FOR THE KINGDOM

Physical balance also means making sure we have time to do the things — work, family, participating in our church or other spiritual groups, doing volunteer work, exercising, playing, being sexually and emotionally active with our spouse, along with all the paid and unpaid activities that make us feel happy and fulfilled. It takes balance in all six aspects of our lives to combine to create a fully balanced person: Physical, mental, emotional, social, financial, and spiritual.

Physical balance also means getting enough sleep every night. I know when I am sleep-deprived I can get more easily distracted, grumpy, and out of sorts for hours until I take a nap or restore that balance. If you have children, you know how they get when their lives are out of balance, If they're hungry, or sleepy, didn't get enough attention, or loving, or proper intellectual stimulation, they get grouchy. They'll scream or cry at the slightest thing. This happens with adults too, only we usually know enough not to let the whole world see it as a toddler might. But we do get short-tempered or grouchy. Those are signs you're out of balance! Learn to watch for them and then adjust what you need to.

Physical balance means staying clean and practicing good hygiene. Remember, our bodies are a temple to God. Habits that impact that temple, be it an excess of food or alcohol, or habits like smoking or vaping, create an imbalance. When you're not clean and haven't bathed, it's like not getting enough sleep. Your body knows and reacts with moodiness or in other ways. Use prayer to help you.

There used to be certain kinds of people who would push me out of balance. I saw one day that being around negative, complaining, energy-sucking people drained me and put me out of balance. Once I began limiting or eliminating those influences in my life, I went back into balance. Look around your life. Is there a co-worker who complains all the time? How do you feel after listening to them vent for 30 minutes? You may not be able to avoid them

Aspect Number Two: Seek A Physical Balance

entirely, but you can limit the amount of time you spend with them.

Saying things like, "I'm so sorry you're going through so much in your life, but I only have five minutes to be a sounding board for you." Set a boundary, then enforce it. If they want to know why you suddenly can't listen to them anymore, tell them about this book, that you're getting your life into balance, and that hearing too much negativity puts you out of balance. They may not like it, but it's the truth. See it as a chance to witness as well as get back in balance.

Our mental well-being is important and the people, drama, and other events in our lives can affect our mental balance. Are you spending time in the Scripture? And are you spending time educating yourself about your job, yourself, and your world? Do you keep up with the news and understand what is happening around you? Do you read? Do you attend Bible studies or events where people are upbeat and positive and worship God? Do you watch documentaries and wholesome movies, and not hours and hours of violence or murder and horror? Our eyes are the windows to our souls, and everything we see, watch, or experience becomes a part of who we are and who we will become.

If you're watching horror movies or porn, or movies that glorify violence and abuse, or even that use curse words, stop. Those will bring you into a state of physical, mental, and psychological, and spiritual imbalance. Studies show that pornography permanently alters the brain and not in a good way. It destroys relationships and our ability to form healthy physical, sexual, and emotional relationships with our spouses or future spouses.

There's a reason God created sex within marriage, and why He details where and how we're to enjoy it — and always within marriage, never outside of it. Sex, as God designed it, isn't bad or evil. Read the Song of Solomon. It's said that Jewish men were not allowed to read the Song of Solomon until they were 30 or about to be married. God only has a problem with sex when it is outside of marriage, and not as He created it to be — a union of husband and wife in love.

Physical balance can mean financial balance and healthy life planning. If you're not a "financial wizard," start with the basics — keeping your bank account balanced, tithing, saving, and paying your bills on time. It may not seem important now, or you may wish you'd started paying attention to your financial life decades ago. It's never too late to start getting this aspect of your physical life in balance.

Do you have a healthy relationship with your possessions? Are you a hoarder, or have a cluttered home, or so much stuff that you're not even sure what you own? God wants us to have a healthy relationship and balance with our possessions. Essentially, He wants us to depend on Him, not on our things. If you have stuff you can't let go of, or that you take great pride in owning, ask yourself if those things are your "gods" rather than God being your primary focus.

Being physically healthy isn't something we achieve in a day or even a decade. It's something we work at every day for our entire lives. If you're young, start now. If you're old, start now. God looks at our hearts and attitudes, not the numbers or amount of things we acquire, win, buy, or own. He wants to know how we've used what He's given us to advance His kingdom.

Of all the aspects of our lives that we need to ensure are balanced, physical balance is probably the hardest because it encompasses so much:

- Our home
- Our physical health
- Our diet
- Our exercise
- Our belongings
- Our family — especially our children

Aspect Number Two: Seek A Physical Balance

- Our activities
- Our walk with God
- Our mental health

It can definitely feel overwhelming. Think about New Year's resolutions and how we try to stick with just one resolution and how challenging that can be! When we try to do too much, we become overwhelmed and don't do anything. Then we feel bad about that and that starts a vicious cycle that discourages us from trying again, from praying, and from seeking God. We just give up.

While I'm sharing all these aspects of life we need to seek balance in, I'm not telling you that you have to do them all at once. The first area of your life that needs balance in your walk with God. You can't do any of the other areas until you're walking with Him and in the Scriptures every day. I don't care if you start with five minutes in prayer and the Word. You have to be feeding yourself with the Word if you're going to get the balance you want. You can do a daily quiet time and spend one minute in prayer, one in worship and gratitude, thanking God for all He's done and is going to do for you. Then spend two minutes reading as much as you can. Don't race through it. If it's a paragraph, then it's a paragraph. Read it thoughtfully, then spend the last minute asking God to reveal His will and His insight about that paragraph. Reflect on the verse(s) all day.

The Word of God is more powerful than you can imagine. All He needs is five minutes of your day, and a commitment from you to learn, to get to know Him, and to listen. He'll do the rest. I guarantee it.

Often the best way to get rid of a bad habit is to replace it with a new habit. Instead of having that soda or sugary cereal for breakfast, swap out the soda with flavored water, and the cereal with some scrambled eggs. Your body and mind are used to you having breakfast, so all you need to do is swap out the bad food for healthy food. It takes us about

SOARING FOR THE KINGDOM

40 days to replace or change a habit but, very importantly, 90 days to master it. At this point of 90 days, you have birthed a new habit. Forty days. Christ went on a 40-day fast before starting His ministry. If He can go without food for 40 days, you can change just one habit. Don't try to change all your habits. Pick one you believe you can change. When that thing is a habit, then pick the next thing and work on it.

Maybe you don't exercise or don't exercise enough. Commit to walking around the block, or down to the corner of your block. If you don't live in a neighborhood where you can walk, or can't walk safely, go to an indoor mall, and walk there. Many malls even have walking programs. Commit to 15-to-30 minutes a day to start. If you can't make it to the end of your driveway, then set a goal to make that happen. Get clearance from your doctor if you need to but take that first step.

I realized years ago, that Christ rarely healed people without requiring them to put forth either faith, or effort, or both. He had the blind man wash mud from his eyes. He had the lepers stretch forth their limbs and commanded the crippled man to stand and take up his blanket and walk.

Christ expected those He helped to be participants in their own healing. He did the hard work, forgave their sins, and renewed their bodies, but He also expected them to have and show faith in His healing. Faith was and is such a critical aspect of our healing that Matthew wrote, *"Now He did not do many mighty works there because of their unbelief." — Matthew 13:58*

Faith in God is a critical element of our balance. We have to believe that God wants to have a relationship with us, that He loves us, that He can and will heal us. Then we have to act on that faith and take the first step. It's not like He's asking us to move mountains, although He gives us the wherewithal to do so with our faith.

Aspect Number Two: Seek A Physical Balance

If we have faith the size of a mustard seed, we can accomplish great things. But where does faith come from? *"So, then faith comes by hearing and hearing by the Word of God,"* (Romans 10:17). See? It all goes back to being in the Word, and our relationship with God. We cannot have faith or sustain faith in God if we're not in His Word. There's a reason He likened the Word to bread, milk, and meat. Food was the one thing everyone understood. There were no grocery stores. People fed themselves through hard work. For Christ to tell them, and in many cases feed them loaves and fishes, that He was food for them, had a much greater impact on them than it does on us.

If I can encourage you to start with one thing, it's to get into the scriptures and read. Begin with the Gospels (Matthew, Mark, Luke, and John). Read them, then go back and reread them until you begin to feel them satisfy your soul. Once you feel the Word feeding and satisfying you, you'll never stop reading it.

SOARING FOR THE KINGDOM

ACTION ITEMS

- **Create a list of areas where you believe, or feel God is showing you that you need to focus on.** Prioritize this list in order of which areas you'll address first. Where do you most need balance? Is it your spiritual life? Your physical life? Set S.M.A.R.T. goals for yourself and get out your calendar and mark them down. Put your calendar where you'll see it every day, preferably when you're having your quiet time. What we focus on improves and grows. When you see your goals in front of you every day, you'll be prodded to make sure you work on them.
- **Find an accountability partner — someone who is reading this book, or willing to read it along with you.** Find someone you trust and can pray with and talk to about each of these chapters. The devil doesn't want you in the Word or developing a relationship with Christ or God. He'll do everything he can to distract and discourage you. Having a strong friend or partner who will be by your side can do wonders. If you are married, your spouse may be that person or one of them. Find someone who you can pray with, talk to, and be accountable. It may take some time but keep praying for the right person. God will bring them into your life. Don't say you "can't change" until you have a partner. Christ will be your partner while you're waiting on another human being. If you have to start alone, then start. God will bring a helper to meet with you.
- **Memorize a verse that inspires and motivates you.** Repeat it and reflect on it daily. Consider this your "daily snack" and a way to chew on the Word. Once you've memorized that verse and have no trouble repeating it, memorize another one. You want to "hide the Word of God in your heart." No one, especially the devil, can take it from

Aspect Number Two: Seek A Physical Balance

your heart, and it will be there in tough times for you to call on. Everyone prefers different kinds of verses but take your time and find the words that speak to you, encourage you, and build you up.

Chapter 8

Aspect Number Three: Seek a Spiritual Balance

I was recently listening to a sermon by a popular pastor who was sharing a story about being on a plane and trying to read his Bible. The man across the aisle from him was a little inebriated and kept wanting to talk, bothering the pastor with chit-chat, asking him about what he was reading.

"The Bible," he answered, saying he knew that put most people off — like waving garlic at a vampire. He hoped the man would be offended and turn away so he could keep reading! But that seemed to be even more attractive to the man, who was now really interested in hearing more about what exactly he was reading in the Bible. The pastor said he kept getting more and more annoyed with the man as the man asked him more and more questions about God and the Bible.

Incredibly, the pastor turned in his seat with his back to the man, then ignored him altogether until he finally turned to tell the man bluntly, "Leave me alone, can't you see I'm reading my Bible?" As he was about to say that, the man asked, "Do you believe in God? Why? What's the Bible say about God anyway?"

Aspect Number Three: Seek a Spiritual Balance

The pastor was stunned and humbled. Here he was so intent on reading his Bible he almost missed a chance to share the Gospel and Jesus Christ. His travel schedule kept him from enjoying what he loved most, reading the Bible and communing with God, so he sought out any time he could read — usually on a flight.

What the pastor forgot was that being open to sharing his passion was why he was a pastor in the first place. I was just amazed. First, that he didn't see the opportunity immediately, then secondly, that he was humble enough to share this event, and third, very grateful he did. He went on to lead the man to Christ and spent the rest of the flight talking about God, Christ, and the Bible.

But what if the pastor had managed to turn the man away before he did? There was the perfect opportunity — a man who wanted to know God and asked him to share what he knew! How could he have NOT seen this man was thirsting for God? Maybe the inebriation turned him off. He might have made other assumptions. I know many Christians who are the opposite — and would have embraced the chance to talk with a fellow passenger rather than read the Word. I'd have probably done what this pastor did, as there's nothing I'd rather do than be in the Word every chance I get. In thinking about his experience, I had some questions for myself.

I wondered how many times in my life I've missed an opportunity to *serve* God because I was so engrossed in *learning* about God. I think this is the perfect example of spiritual imbalance.

There's nothing wrong with spending every waking minute praying, reading the Scriptures, or being involved with God — unless it interferes with our other responsibilities and life. When we become so focused on God that we can't see or sense His other children, and His commandments to us to share, preach, feed, clothe and visit the sick and needy, we're out of balance. We need to be living our lives, working, going to school, raising children, and doing whatever we need to do while at the same time loving God.

SOARING FOR THE KINGDOM

A healthy, spiritually balanced Christian is also led by the Holy Spirit, listens to God's guidance and teachings, and is led by the Holy Spirit moment by moment. When we do this long enough, it becomes second nature. We don't have to think about it, we just do it.

God tells us to, "Love the Lord with all your heart and with all your soul and with all your mind," (Matthew 22:37-39). Yet, immediately after that, the Bible says, "Love your neighbor as yourself." Loving God is a spiritual focus, and loving our neighbor is a natural focus. When we can love God and our neighbor and be present in both the spiritual realm and the natural or physical realm, we're living a life of balance. There will be times we need to put our physical demands ahead of our spiritual demands, wants, and needs — in ways that fulfill God's plans for us. Just as the pastor wanted to be left alone to read his Bible, God wanted him to set aside that "spiritual time" to be physically hands-on and share the Gospel with a man looking to understand and ultimately accept Christ.

God isn't looking for a legalistic approach to spiritual balance. He's not looking for us to say, "Okay, I'll spend x-number of hours in church, or the Word, or praying, and then I'll do my other things, like work and family." You can't make "spiritual balance" a chore or an item on your to-do list. God wants us all, 100 percent of the day, yet He expects us to be "in the world" and take care of our jobs, family, school, and whatever else we have going on. He wants a balance. So how do you give God 100 percent of you while also giving your life what it needs?

> *"Rejoice always, pray without ceasing, give thanks in all circumstances; for this is the will of God in Christ Jesus for you."*
>
> *— 1 Thessalonians 5:16-18*

Aspect Number Three: Seek a Spiritual Balance

Spiritual balance means having an awareness of God and His actions in our lives no matter where we are or what we're doing. It means trusting Him, turning to Him, listening, meditating on, and being grateful to Him no matter what.

Consider the story of Aleisha. She often shared with others that she was in constant contact with God during difficult times, and there were plenty of those times. You see Aleisha lived in Punta Cana where there were armed guards with rifles in front of every storefront. So when she had to go shopping, instead of seeing these guards and thinking, "Oh, I hope nothing happens." Or "I hope I don't get shot!" Instead, she started saying quietly and consistently, "Thank you, God for your constant protection."

Aleisha added, "We all think thousands of thoughts daily—thoughts that often are fear focused. But when I began turning my thoughts to God into prayers of gratitude, I was able to calm my fears and, as a result, feel God's abiding love wrap around me like a warm blanket." Aleisha's abiding faith proved to be contagious. People who happened to walk with her when she went shopping shared with her that they felt a rich sense of calm and peace were before, they felt an imbalance and the fear that comes with not having a personal relationship with God.

Balance, I've learned, is not like a see-saw or a set of scales where one thing is heavier than another, causing the scales to go out of balance. Balance is front-to-back, side-to-side, outside-to-inside, and so on. It's all directions, so it's not as simple as it may seem. Balance is complex. It's a mix of your relationship with God and with various aspects of yourself into a way of being, living, and acting in a way that brings us peace and calm no matter what is happening around us.

How is that possible!? I hear from others. There's too much to think about! Well, at first, there is a lot to think about. Then a spiritual focus becomes a part of you. It becomes natural, second nature almost, to say a prayer as you're getting in the car or sending your

SOARING FOR THE KINGDOM

children off to school for the day. Our spiritual focus becomes part of us, our thoughts, our awareness, and our emotions.

Being spiritually balanced means being connected with the people and purposes in our lives as well. Are you physically healthy? Are you mentally healthy? Are you confessing sin and "keeping short accounts with God" to stay in communion with Him? Are you avoiding gossip, negative people, and negative situations that can pull you into "poverty thinking?" Poverty thinking isn't just thinking there's not enough money or financial balance in your life. You can have poverty thinking about relationships, opportunities (nothing ever good ever happens to me), and people (I don't have any good friendships).

Are you avoiding the 24/7 negativity of the news, social media, and your friends and co-workers? Bad things happen, and we must deal with them, but there's no reason to surround yourself with gossips, busybodies, and negative people.

Are you celebrating the "mini-miracles" in your life? They happen every day. Maybe you're late to work or a meeting, and a parking spot opens up right in front of where you need to go. You may order lunch and get double portions because the kitchen has run out of enough of the item you ordered, so you got the extra. Maybe you pull up to a parking meter, and there's almost an hour's worth of time left on it. Or you find a dollar bill on the sidewalk. These don't seem like much in the grand scheme of things, but I call them "mini-miracles" because they make me happy and remind me God is aware of what I'm going through.

While I was writing this book, I heard a story from my editor about a man named Troy who was a Christian, but who believed that God and spirituality were "too formal and dressy" for someone like him. He wanted to know God understood and loved him and cared about him. He was scheduled for surgery for a non-life-threatening health issue. He was nervous about the surgery, and as he was being taken to

Aspect Number Three: Seek a Spiritual Balance

his room, he said, jokingly, "If God really loves me, He'll have Doritos and a cherry Coke waiting for me." He was joking, but God was not.

A few steps later, they entered the room and there on the table beside the bed was a six-pack of cherry Cokes and a huge bag of Doritos. No one knew who put them there, but ever since that day, Troy has never doubted God's love for him.

God does know our tiniest preferences and exactly what makes us happy, no matter how small a thing we think it is. What parent has not bought a small toy or snack for their child, knowing how much they love it, or has remembered their favorite cartoon character or hobby, be it flowers, bugs, or dinosaurs, when buying clothing with such items on it?

God's not out of touch with us. He longs to give us the desires of our hearts — no matter how large or small and to be with us, for us to turn to Him with anything and everything going on in our lives.

ACTION ITEMS

- **Define what spiritual balance means to you.**
  Don't compare yourself to your friends or others in your life.
  This is all about you and your spiritual balance. God does
  not ask or expect us to be "number one" or race to better
  others with our lives. He wants us to be balanced, available
  and doing our best for Him and no one else.
- **Take time to assess *your* spiritual balance.**
  Remember, MORE time in the Word or at church does not
  indicate spiritual balance. Do you feel like you're spending
  as much time in the Word or praying or in communion with
  God as you'd like? Do you feel guilty for not spending more
  time with God because other things are more important to
  you? What do you think you need to do to get back in
  balance spiritually?
- **On two index cards, write down three things you
  know that show or tell you you're out of balance
  and three that show you're in balance.** Post these
  lists where you can read them often. You may also put them
  in your Bible or use them as bookmarks. Just make sure you
  read and refer to them until they become part of you.

Chapter 9

Aspect Number Four: Seek a Social Balance

Jesus didn't have any social media accounts, but He was and is a social creature. He had friends among the lowest and highest members of society. If He'd had a YouTube, Twitter, or other social media channel, He would have had millions or billions of followers. Yet, even without any technology, and only a small group of 12 men, one of whom betrayed Him, He has the largest following, and the greatest influence of anyone in history. So how did He do it? One person, or one small group or small community at a time.

He utilized the principle of small group communities and a social circle that varied from three or four disciples to 12 disciples, depending on His purpose. Not all the disciples, for instance, accompanied Him to the mountain of transfiguration. Only Peter, James, and John, the brother of James, joined Christ on the mountain.

> *"Jesus, Peter, James, and John, the brother of James, went up on a high mountain by themselves. While they watched, Jesus' appearance was changed; his face became bright like*

SOARING FOR THE KINGDOM

*the sun, and his clothes became white as light. Then Moses
and Elijah appeared to them, talking with Jesus."*

— *Matthew 17:2-3*

So, while Jesus had 12 disciples, not all of them were part of His inner circle or privy to everything He had to say. Some disciples are never mentioned after they joined Christ as a disciple, and some are mentioned only infrequently. Yet, Christ connected with and worked with all of them.

Experts tell us that the most people we can have in a small, intimate, close circle of friends is about five people. We can't manage more than that many close friendships. There isn't enough time in the day or our schedules to tend to more than that effectively and lovingly.

We can have a social circle of about 150 (Dunbar's number) and possibly a closer social circle of about 10-15, but the real number of friends, the deep circle, is five.

I'm reminded of the parable of the talents, where a master entrusted his servants with different amounts of gold. To one, he gives five talents, to another three, and another, one talent. He then goes on his journey. The first two men invest their gold and double the amount, but the one given the least amount of gold, one talent, merely buries it in the ground and does nothing with it. The master is pleased when he returns and sees his servants have invested wisely. Then he asks the servant who buried his talent why he didn't invest it.

The man replied, "I knew that you are a hard man, harvesting where you have not sown and gathered where you have not scattered seed. So, I was afraid and went out and hid your gold in the ground. See, here is what belongs to you." The master was furious and took the man's one talent and gave it to the man to whom he had given five talents and then said, "You wicked, lazy servant! So, you knew that I harvest where I have not sown and gather where I have not scattered

Aspect Number Four: Seek a Social Balance

seed? Well then, you should have put my money on deposit with the bankers so that when I returned, I would have received it back with interest."

> *"So, take the bag of gold from him and give it to the one who has ten bags. For whoever has will be given more, and they will have an abundance. Whoever does not have, even what they have will be taken from them. And throw that worthless servant outside, into the darkness, where there will be weeping and gnashing of teeth."*
>
> — *Matthew 25:14–30*

Most of us don't think about our social influence being part of the "talents" God has given us, yet that's exactly what our presence in the world is — a talent waiting to be invested. We have the potential to invest in our social media presence and make a difference for the Kingdom. Fortunately, thanks to Facebook and other social media, being social is not an issue. Being "too" social or out of balance socially can be an issue. Are you "burying" your talent in the ground and only using social media to promote yourself and your interests? Or are you reaching non-believers with your posts and interactions?

How much time do you spend on social media? What are you doing there? Posting, gossiping, keeping up, or competing with "friends?" Is the time you spend on social media enhancing or detracting from your time with God, or in the Word? Are you making healthy contacts there? I'm not judging. I'm asking you to examine your life and whether you're balanced in all areas.

Today, "social balance" is often seen as a critical part of your social media presence. Who are you on Twitter, Facebook, Instagram, or other social media platforms? How well do you connect with and influence others? If someone "accused" you of being a born-again

SOARING FOR THE KINGDOM

believer, would your followers have no problem confirming that you are? Or do your posts sound like any other post?

Fortunately, technology can help even the shyest and non-social people among us gain an audience and a following. But what does it mean to seek a social balance? Should we be gathering followers and chasing down millions of subscribers? Is that what God wants? Many of the popular pastors have followers in the millions. What are they doing with their influence? The goal is not, as most of us think, to have the greatest number of followers or fans. The goal is to make an impact with the people we do reach.

Christ only had 12 disciples, yet they changed the world. God works in small social circles and communities, not big ones. When He sent the disciples out to witness to different towns, He sent them in pairs. Two men, the smallest community possible, and it worked. When they returned to Christ, they were jubilant and told of casting out demons and healing the sick.

Part of the reason Jesus sent them out in pairs had to do with Old Testament law (Deut. 19:15) and the law that at least two witnesses were needed to convict someone of a crime. Plus, two witnesses are more believable than one and more likely to be listened to. I like those reasons, but I still believe Jesus was thinking of the power of shared ministry. When one falls, another will pick him up and encourage him.

> *"For if they fall, one will lift his companion. But woe to him who is alone when he falls, For he has no one to help him up."*

> — *Ecclesiastes 4:10*

So, while the Bible never mentions or uses the words "support circles," the concept is there. The number-one way people

Aspect Number Four: Seek a Social Balance

communicated during Christ's time was through talking, reading the Torah, and letters. Most Hebrews studied with the rabbis. Since the rabbi's job was to teach and maintain religious and cultural standards, literacy was important to the Jews. To preserve the identity of the Jewish nation, as many men and women as possible needed to be able to read.

However, the vast majority of the Gentiles were illiterate — up to 98 percent — some experts say. So, the letters the disciples wrote had to be read to the Gentile followers, who would then memorize the contents and discuss them among themselves.

Unlike "reading" today, the Jews also needed to understand history, literature, philosophy, and the culture of their religion to preserve it. That's how Judaism was able to survive 2,600 years of exile. Once every boy or girl "came of age" and had their bar mitzvah (boys) or bat mitzvah (girls). They were expected to be able to read from the Torah during this ceremony. They couldn't just memorize a passage from the Torah. They didn't know what they would be reading until the rabbi opened the scroll. So, it's very likely most Jews were literate and more aware of history than the average Gentile or Roman citizen.

The Bereans, a Jewish sect who were more open-minded than many of the Jews the disciples encountered, were eager to learn as much as they could about God, which is why *"they received the Word with all eagerness, examining the Scriptures daily to see if these things were so." — Acts 17:11.*

And, while Paul, a Jew, wasn't one of the original disciples, he did write seven of the 27 books of the New Testament. 1 Thessalonians, 1 Corinthians, 2 Corinthians, Galatians, Philippians, and Romans, and while many attribute at least 13 books to Paul, these are the only ones that can be authenticated as being written by him.

Paul, like most Jews, was not illiterate. He was more religiously educated than any of the disciples. In Acts 22:3, Paul claims that he studied under the great Pharisaic teacher, Gamaliel, who may have been the grandson of Hillel the Elder (sometimes noted as one of the great proto-rabbis [often called "sages" or "teachers"] of the first century BCE). He was also born a Roman citizen, a very high status that granted him rights and privileges that most of the citizens of the time did not have:

PAUL THE ROMAN CITIZEN

"The crowd listened to Paul until he said this. Then they raised their voices and shouted, "Rid the earth of him! He's not fit to live!" As they were shouting and throwing off their cloaks and flinging dust into the air[2], the commander ordered that Paul be taken into the barracks. He directed that he be flogged and interrogated to find out why the people were shouting at him like this. As they stretched him out to flog him, Paul said to the centurion standing there, "Is it legal for you to flog a Roman citizen who hasn't even been found guilty?" When the centurion heard this, he went to the commander and reported it. "What are you going to do?" he asked. "This man is a Roman citizen."

The commander went to Paul and asked, "Tell me, are you a Roman citizen?"

"Yes, I am," he answered.

Then the commander said, "I had to pay a lot of money for my citizenship."

"But I was born a citizen," Paul replied. Those who were about to interrogate him withdrew immediately. The commander himself was alarmed when he realized that he had put Paul, a Roman citizen, in chains."

Since Paul also studied under Gamaliel, one of the most respected teaching lineages in the late Second Temple period, he seems to have been educated beyond simple Torah expertise. His understanding of

Aspect Number Four: Seek a Social Balance

the Prophets and classical literature and philosophy was matched only by his passion for serving God. In today's terms, Paul would have been considered "an influencer" on social media. An influencer is someone who has the respect, following, and power to influence others — as he certainly did — and without the social media technology we use today.

The other thing Paul had was a high EQ that enabled him to talk to people and share the gospel in ways they understood, remembered, and shared with their friends and family.

You don't need to be a genius or even all that smart to be a successful, wise, or powerful leader. But you do need to have a high EQ (Emotional Intelligence). Social expertise is measured by something called "emotional intelligence," which is the ability to understand, use, and manage your own emotions in positive ways to relieve stress, communicate effectively, empathize with others, overcome challenges, and defuse conflict. Emotional intelligence helps you build stronger relationships, succeed at school and work, and achieve your career and personal goals. It can also help you to connect with your feelings, turn intention into action, and make informed decisions about what matters most to you. Leaders are social people, and EQ requires good social skills, awareness, and understanding of people, their emotions, and one's own emotions.

> *"A man who isolates himself seeks his own desire; He rages against all wise judgment."*
>
> — *Proverbs 18:1-11*

CIRCLES OF SUPPORT

Following Christ is all about building community. It's the very first thing He did before starting His ministry. He gathered a community of disciples around Him. After He had risen, His disciples continued

SOARING FOR THE KINGDOM

to stress the importance of community as an integral part of being a follower and maintaining their faith.

> *"And let us consider one another in order to stir up love and good works, not forsaking the assembling of ourselves together, as is the manner of some, but exhorting one another, and so much the more as you see the day approaching."*
>
> — *Hebrews 10:24-25*

At the time Paul wrote this, he did not mean, "Don't stop attending church." There was no church at that time. Believers met in groups in each other's homes or wherever they could. He meant don't forsake the community and support of other believers. He understood the strength and hope to be found in gathering together to encourage each other, to teach and learn from each other, and to belong to a like-minded group of believers.

People like to feel a part of something. A community is not the same as a team. It's not about ten players and five on the bench with five on the floor. That's a team concept. You are there, but you may not participate. You may not feel as important as some others. But when you speak of community, that's all about building each other and looking out for the betterment of each other, wanting the best for each other. Christ encouraged small circles. He had His 12 disciples, and in that group of 12, He had His small circle of threes — Peter, James, and John. They were the three who witnessed the most astounding of Christ's miracles.

I believe in and want to amplify the need for a small, tight-knit, and supportive community I call "Circles of Support." Over time, I've experienced the power of small groups of supportive Christians. There's just something about having another or a small group of three to five other believers you can share with, pray with, and encourage.

Aspect Number Four: Seek a Social Balance

Any larger than that, the group will demand too much of your time and take you away from your most crucial small circle — your family.

And, as much as many of us would like to believe we can have "dozens and hundreds of friends," it's just not possible.

Malcolm Gladwell, an author and journalist who writes about patterns and business, said in his book, *The Tipping Point*, that as a social scientist, you can't have any more than 15 connected relationships in your life at once. If you count your immediate family, your birth family, and a few extra friends you know from work or church, your friendship card is full.

Jesus never intended for His disciples to gather a "following" of thousands of people who they would then tend to, much as the modern mega-churches do today. He encouraged small groups who then witnessed and discipled other individuals who then started their own groups.

Having a core group, who then disciples and trains others, who in turn start their own small groups and encourage them to do the same, is precisely how and why the Gospel of Christ has spread around the world as it has.

Like communities, these "small circles" are never-ending. People cannot bail out on their community once a commitment is made because it's a circle, and circles are continuous. They have no beginning or ending. It just keeps going. It's almost like a game of jump rope. Once you jump in, you're in. While I love my church and love attending it and all the people I know and enjoy, I do have a small community of women I focus on.

I've been in several different Christian support groups through the years. What they have taught me and shown me was the phenomenon of growing a network. Where has there been the most expansive, diverse, unique network than what's happened with Christianity? Small groups of committed Christians who supported each other spawned support circles that created more small circles. The world is all about numbers and the number of followers and getting more views, likes, and fans. At no time in His ministry did Christ ever focus on followers. He cared only that people heard about the Gospel.

He never chased people down or begged them to follow Him. He spoke the truth and what they chose from there on out was up to them. When Judas was in the process of betraying Him, Christ knew. It wasn't a surprise. He knew when He chose Judas as a disciple that he would sell Him for 30 pieces of silver. Still, He encouraged and supported and tried to help Judas see the truth, but He couldn't. Judas betraying Christ was a necessary act for salvation to take place and Jesus knew it. It saddened Him deeply, but He understood.

Betrayal happens in small groups, too. We're all sinners and humans, but in a small group, it's much more likely people will be less likely to spiral out of control. But if they do, then it's a lesson for everyone in the group. What I love most about small groups though, is there's love, there's care, there's looking after one another, and there's communication. You go through the ups and downs, but you do not forsake your community.

When you're part of a small community, people notice when you're not there. There's accountability and a feeling of being responsible to others. And there are more chances to serve. I've learned that when someone feels like they're a part of the community, they're just waiting for the opportunity to arise where they can jump in. They feel a part of something bigger than themselves. That's what community is all about. They tell me, "I feel a part of something important. I know I'm cared for and that someone is there for me, and I have the opportunity to reciprocate and be there for someone else."

That's a true community. We forgive, we have our ups and our downs, we forgive, we keep going, we have some tough conversations, and we challenge each other. We are there to convict each other, to

Aspect Number Four: Seek a Social Balance

inspire and encourage each other — that's what community is about. It's a force of mental, physical, spiritual, and emotional well-being.

So many people are looking for this, but they don't realize how important it would be for someone to invite them in. "Hey, would you please come in? We consider you a valued community member to share your best skills and ...."

It's not just a place to shine and show off your strengths. It's a place to share your strengths and your weaknesses. There's a family feel to it, so you feel safe. And that's the point. You're supposed to feel secure and comfortable and able to be vulnerable with the others in your group.

SOARING FOR THE KINGDOM

ACTION ITEMS

- **Take an inventory of your closest friends.** Who are they, what do they believe, and are they active, passionate Christians? We can have non-believers and lukewarm believers in our circles — it's practically impossible not to. But the people we have around us, the ones we lean on, spend most of our time with, and look to for mutual support and encouragement, should be at least as passionate about God and Jesus Christ as we are. We become who we associate with.

- **Evaluate your social media and the amount of time you spend on it.** Are you spending more than an hour a day on Facebook, Twitter, Instagram, Telegram, or whatever your favorite media site is? Is it productive and brings you into contact with more believers? Or is it a place to gossip, brag, and chill? There's nothing wrong with connecting with other believers. God wants us to. He does not want us to be busybodies, gossips, or time wasters on social media. That sounds harsh, I know. I'm not saying to give up social media. I'm asking only that you evaluate whether it's advancing your relationship with Christ. Only you can answer that. If you're not sure of the answer, ask God. Trust me. He'll let you know if you ask Him honestly for His input.

Chapter 10

Aspect Number Five — Seek a Psychological Balance

A while back, my husband and I were in a restaurant, eating dinner, and enjoying our time together when we heard a huge crash and the sound of plates and glasses breaking. A young waiter had lost control of his tray and it became unbalanced, sending food, plates, and glasses crashing to the ground. His coworkers moved quickly to help him clean up the mess, reassuring him that they too, had dropped trays and it was "no big deal." He thanked them profusely, but his voice was quaking, and tears stung his eyes. He might laugh about it later, but right now, it was embarrassing and painful for him, and uncomfortable for others who witnessed it. Some felt bad for him, some felt critical — assuming he must be incompetent to drop a tray. Some ignored the crash, perhaps preferring not to add to his discomfort. I felt empathy for him, having experienced public embarrassment myself when I've done something wrong.

I'm sure it was worse in my mind than in the minds of others, just as he felt more shame than those around him trying to reassure him. By the next day, or possibly even within his shift, if he is a healthy, normal human being, with a sound psychological balance, he will be able to laugh about dropping the tray or even joke about it. If he's not psychologically balanced, he may worry about the incident for days, or even weeks and months. He may "beat himself up," by telling himself how clumsy or stupid, or incompetent he is. None of that is true, but it's what we say when we aren't as balanced as we could be. He may even quit his job to ensure he never again drops another tray or feels that level of shame.

The difference in whether or not he can "shake it off," and go back to work, or dwell on the event is in his psychological makeup — which includes his confidence and self-esteem levels, and how he perceives the events that happen to him.

Psychology is the study of the mind and people's behavior and personality traits. The same thing can happen to a dozen people and each of them will perceive it differently, — psychologically, emotionally, and even physically, based upon our psychology — meaning our thoughts, behavior, development, personality, emotion, motivation, and more.

Each of the disciples had a different personality and psychology. Jesus called James and John, the "Sons of Thunder," possibly based on their personalities and response during an occasion when Jesus attempted to find accommodations for the night. He tried one place, but the villagers denied Him. He was met with much opposition due to the existing Jew-Samaritan prejudice because His destination was Jerusalem.

When James and John saw this, they asked, "Lord, do you want us to call fire down from Heaven to destroy them?" The two men were generally quick to anger and to judge. Raining down fire to destroy some villagers was a pretty intense response to being denied accommodations.

Then there was Peter — open mouth, insert foot, Peter. When Peter accompanied Jesus to the Mount of Transfiguration and saw Moses,

Aspect Number Five — Seek a Psychological Balance

Jesus, and Elijah, his response was, "Let's build everyone a tent." Now, Jesus is shining more brightly than the sun, and there are two dead prophets with Him, and all Peter can think of is putting up some tents. He was the first to leap out of the boat and walk on water, yet also looked down and realized what was happening, and sank. He denied Christ after saying he "would never." He was quite the personality. I often wonder how I would have reacted in those same situations.

Thomas, forever famous not so much for how he ministered, but as much as how he doubted Christ's resurrection. Even today, a "doubting Thomas" is a name given to skeptics who refuse to believe without direct personal experience — a reference to the Gospel of John's depiction of the Apostle Thomas. In John's account, Thomas refused to believe the resurrected Jesus had appeared to the 10 other apostles until he could see and feel Jesus' crucifixion wounds for himself.

> *"So the other disciples told him, 'We have seen the Lord.' But he [Thomas] said to them, 'Unless I see in his hands the mark of the nails, and place my finger into the mark of the nails, and place my hand into his side, I will never believe.'"*
>
> *— John 20:25-31*

I can understand how he might have felt. When things happen to us, it's always more powerful, more believable, and more moving than when we hear about something. I've read or seen news reports of other young women and girls who have been victims of an assault and saddened by their experience, and I felt moved to pray for them. I never felt or identified with what was happening until it happened to my daughter. It rocked my world — not nearly as much as hers, but I was devastated. I think I may have preferred it happened to me than her because she has anxiety and a condition doctors label a "mental illness." Yet, it struck me how easily we move past others' trauma and crisis without truly understanding.

I had never thought about what it must have taken for other women and girls to get through an attack, and now here I am, faced with that thing. And I am trying to find where my husband and I can best support our daughter during this time. I'm off-balance, trying to find my balance, trying to depend on Jesus to help me center my soul and be calm as I work to restore us all to some sense of normal while we all heal.

Psychological balance is knowing what you're capable of and what's nearly impossible for you to do, and I'm learning a great deal about where I fall short. Going back to the example in the restaurant, what I found so calming was hearing this young waiter's coworkers reassuring him that he wasn't the first and wouldn't be the last to lose a tray or his balance. As we continued to eat, we heard bits and pieces of the stories that followed. Someone shared their embarrassing story about slipping and falling on a wet floor with a tray of drink glasses, another was bumped by a clumsy customer, another was rushing to serve her tables on a busy evening ... I listened to their stories. I realized we all lose our balance at some time.

Maybe we don't carry heavy food trays, but we often struggle with other psychological balances — how to be a "good Christian witness" and not to lose it and yell or be short-tempered with others. It's a balancing act, and there are plenty of days when we're too tired, too hot, too cold, too frustrated, and too short-tempered to be "balanced." Like the waiter who lost control of his tray, we lose control of our temper, words, and emotions. Everything we're doing goes crashing down. We may destroy, chip, or break relationships or stain our reputation. We've lost our balance, and now we have the wreckage we created to clean up.

Aspect Number Five — Seek a Psychological Balance

We may get up and run out of a meeting crying or hold on to our dignity long enough to get to the restroom or our car before we cry and "lose it," but the imbalance is still there.

We can be off-balance psychologically by becoming too emotional or not being emotional enough. Remember Goldilocks and the three bears? She went from chair to chair, and bed to bed, searching "for just the right one" — the "right balance."

In our quest to be the best mother, father, daughter, son, parent, friend, or employee, we're often balancing a lot of feelings, thoughts, fears, and actions. We can lose our psychological balance because we're tired, worried, angry, scared, frightened, frustrated, or offended. A co-worker, friend, or spouse may be more demanding or needy than usual. We may not feel well. We may have more happening in our lives than we can handle. We begin to worry more about what others think of us than what God thinks of us.

When we are off-balance more than we're centered or balanced, then that becomes a problem. Satan loves nothing more than to see us reeling about, unable or unwilling to rein in our minds and our emotions.

I'm not saying "peak experiences" are bad. They can be wonderful and memorable, and enriching. Who hasn't enjoyed peak experiences like the birth of a child or grandchild, graduation, a wedding, a job promotion, or a new car or home? These "highs" are what make life worth living. We truly feel free, connected, grateful, and thankful.

On the other hand, all of us will suffer loss in our lives — another extreme emotional experience. A child, spouse, parent, or friend will die or be diagnosed with a terminal illness. We may be bullied, gossiped about, rejected, or have a partner cheat on us or ask for a divorce. We may become physically disabled by an accident or disease. We may lose our jobs or be turned down for a job we thought should have been ours. Is that good? Yes. Extreme experiences shouldn't upset our psychological balance, yet they do. Our goal should never to be rocked by life but to return to the creator of balance — God — when we are.

A balanced life is not disrupted by the extremes but rather enriched by them. God doesn't tell us to seek or avoid extremes. He only asks that we trust Him in whatever situation we find ourselves in. Flexibility and resilience are signs we have found a balance when things go right or wrong. As Paul said to the Philippians:

> *"I am not saying this because I am in need, for I have learned to be content whatever the circumstances. I know what it is to be in need, and I know what it is to have plenty. I have learned the secret of being content in any and every situation, whether well fed or hungry, whether living in plenty or in want. I can do all this through him who gives me strength."*
>
> *— Philippians 4:11-13*

God made us in His image, and that includes His emotions. Throughout the Bible, we read about God being patient, angry, grieved, generous, gracious, and enraged. He gave us emotions to be able to recognize where we are and what decisions to make.

King David was depressed, ashamed, grief-stricken, joyful, happy, content, angry, and lustful — he felt everything we do! Christ felt emotions yet did not sin. He became angry and made a whip and chased the money lenders out of the Temple. He was tired. He was hungry. He was frustrated when His disciples could not stay awake and pray with Him the evening before His arrest by the Romans. He understands. Feeling emotions is not sinful. What we do with those emotions, what we think about, and how we act as a result of those emotions is what makes us unbalanced and more likely to feel distanced from God or sin.

Aspect Number Five — Seek a Psychological Balance

Psychological imbalances are more likely when the other aspects of our life are out of balance. When all of our aspects are functioning in healthy and God-honoring ways, our emotional and psychological balance is healthy.

IS PSYCHOLOGY BIBLICAL?

One of the questions I'm asked is whether the Bible (and God) "approves" of psychology or psychologists. Isn't the Bible and God's work enough for us? Yes and no. The Bible does warn us about turning to the world's wisdom, but only when it contradicts God's Word and wisdom. Psalm 1:1-2; Isa. 55:8-11; Jer. 2:13; 1 Cor. 1:18-2:16

As Christians, we are to depend solely on God and His Word as our support and wisdom in the trials of life (see Psalms 19:7-11; 32:6-11; 33:6-22; 119) so that He alone gets the glory (Ps. 115; Isa. 42:8). An excellent Christian psychologist knows this and has a solid foundation in biblical principles so they can apply God's Word and counsel to psychological issues. Not all psychological problems come from our minds. At times, there are demonic influences. It takes a wise Christian counselor who is in the Word and walks with God to discern spiritual issues from mental and psychological ones.

"Fear not," God tells us in 365 places in Scripture not to be afraid and not to be frightened. He wants us to trust Him and have faith in Him and his plans for us. Fear is the most common emotion we all experience and the one emotion that can separate us from God because it so strongly impacts our faith. "But without faith, it is impossible to please Him: for he that cometh to God must believe that he is and that he is a rewarder of them that diligently seek Him " (Hebrews 11:6). Having a psychological balance is critical.

There are people with hormonal, genetic, and other conditions that require medicine. Are they not Christians because they turn to science and medicine? Of course not! The Apostle Luke was a physician.

For this book, the psychological balance we should seek involves one of mental and spiritual clarity and awareness. Do you know yourself? Do you know your strengths and weaknesses? Are you open to feedback and criticism from trusted friends who truly know you? Are you working to become a better person, one who is gaining respect and stature with God, Christ, and others?

Aspect Number Five — Seek a Psychological Balance

ACTION ITEMS

- **Write down all the things you hate about your body and then thank God for each and every one. Do this daily.** In time you will be incredibly grateful for all He has given you physically and you'll also feel better psychologically about yourself. All of us, even the most seemingly "perfect" people, have psychological issues to some degree. Some may feel ugly or fat, or too tall, too short, or too something. But remember, God made you exactly as he wanted you to be. If you need to gain or lose weight to be physically healthy, that's on you. But every hair and cell of your body is by God's design.

- **Some mental or psychological issues are hard to spot in ourselves.** You may need to see a therapist or mental health expert for a definitive diagnosis. Chances are that you suffer from the same psychological issues most of us do — depression, low self-esteem, anxiety, fear, poor boundaries, codependency, addiction (includes shopping, food, and overwork as well as the usual drug, alcohol, sex, porn, and gambling), and lack of confidence. Write down what psychological issues you struggle with. Turn them over to God, and then begin learning more about them through a combination of Bible study about who you are in Christ, and seeking out Christian self-help books and groups who will help you become who Christ intended you to be.

- **Write down who you would be, what your life would look like if you were a mentally balanced person.** Would you have more friends or fewer? Would you be more confident? Would you have a better-paying job? Would you be in a relationship or a better relationship? What does mental health mean to you? Describing ourselves as mentally healthy can often reveal what we believe we lack in terms of mental health now.

Chapter 11

Aspect Number Six — Seek a Purpose Balance

"Follow me." That's pretty much all Jesus said to each of the disciples when He called them to be part of His mission. There was no explanation, no interview, no discussion, just a declaration to "follow me." He didn't have a "type" of person he was looking for. He asked fishermen, a tax collector, and others to join Him. So why did they leave a family business, a family, a career, their lives, and follow Him?

As devout Jews, they saw the opportunity of a lifetime and jumped on it. Jesus was no stranger to them. Even if they didn't know Him personally, they knew who He was — a rabbi — and a well-known and respected one at that. Being Jewish and having studied the Torah as all observant Jews did at the time, they were talmidim — basic students and potential apprentices to any rabbi. Because the law was taught orally in those days, talmidim would seek out a respected rabbi and ask them to teach them the Torah, the law, and how to implement it. But rabbis only accepted the most promising students. All others had to do what they could — attending temple and listening and learning on their own.

Aspect Number Six — Seek a Purpose Balance

The men Jesus selected knew very well that a Messiah had been promised. To be able to study with Jesus was an incredible opportunity. He was not just a rabbi, He was the rabbi of all rabbis — the Son of God! He was a rabbi who would have been sought out by the brightest and most intelligent potential students asking Him if they could be His apprentice.

For a rabbi of Christ's reputation to approach a talmidim, and say, "Follow me," it meant He believed that the potential talmid had the ability and commitment to become like Him.[1] His disciples recognized Christ was likely the Messiah. In John 1:41, the first thing Andrew did was, *"He first found his own brother Simon, and said to him, "We have found the Messiah" (which is translated, the Christ).* Unlike most of us today, the Jews of Christ's time were looking for the Messiah. Their lives revolved around His appearance. They were expecting Him. So when Jesus walked up to His disciples and said, "Follow me," They had no problem dropping everything to follow Him.

However, Jesus the carpenter was not a stranger or an unknown in the area. He was a very prominent figure in Galilee, and extremely well educated and respected. He had already amazed and astounded rabbis at the Temple as a boy of 12, and in the 18 years since then, He had "only grown in wisdom and stature with men and God."

Jesus had a purpose. His disciples had a purpose, and everything they did for three years was for a reason — to teach, to preach, to heal, and to train those men for life after His death and resurrection. Remember, Jesus' mission only lasted three short years, and He knew exactly when His "time" would begin and when and how it would end. When His mother asked Him to take care of the wine shortage at the wedding in Canaan, He already had His disciples, but as He told her, "My time is not yet come," He acted and His time began. His disciples didn't just join Him and give up everything to follow Him around. They knew who He was and they wanted to be part of

139

SOARING FOR THE KINGDOM

His purpose, whatever it was. They only knew He promised to make them "fishers of men," yet they hoped He was the King who would rule over Jerusalem.

Christ is still asking us to "follow" Him. Yet how many of us say, as many others did to Christ, "Sir, first let me go and bury my father." Now, Christ's response may seem callous, but I recently learned that the man's father had not even died yet! The son was saying he wanted to go home and live comfortably until his father died in the future. The traditional Jewish customs for burial, once someone had died, meant days of preparation, and even weeks and months, up to a year, to bury someone properly. But this man's father hadn't even died yet! Christ knew that the man was not serious about following Him. His rebuke of the man is not about actually burying his father who was already dead. It's about the man wanting the comfort and familiarity of his life and prioritizing his comfort over following the Messiah.

I'd say most of us are a lot like this man — not willing to give up everything, comfort, jobs, money, and our future to follow Christ — knowing the journey will be difficult and very uncomfortable most of the time. We like our comfort. We're willing to commit to a greater good and purpose, but only if we can fit it into our existing life. Have you ever turned down attending a Bible study, or Bible class, or event to stay home and watch your favorite television show? Have you ever turned off the alarm clock and rolled over to get another hour of sleep and go to the second service rather than the first?

How many of us have wrestled with the decision about whether God "wanted us" to get a certain job, or pursue a certain career? How did we decide? The thing is, God can use you no matter what your career or job choice is. He can use you if you're unemployed or on welfare. He can use you no matter what your situation or circumstances are as long as your purpose and attitude are to edify others and glorify Him. That's what He's looking for — a believer who puts Him first in their

140

Aspect Number Six – Seek a Purpose Balance

life. God has a purpose for you. David writes in Psalm 57:2 and says, *"I cry out to God Most High, to God who fulfills his purpose for me."*

God is a God of purpose. He designed you before you were even conceived, which includes His knowing where He wanted you and what He wanted you doing. *"Before I formed you in the womb I knew you, and before you were born, I consecrated you; I appointed you as a prophet to the nations."* (Jer. 1:5). And if we mess up that purpose (impossible), no problem. He says in Romans 8:28, *"And we know that in all things God works for the good of those who love him, who have been called according to his purpose." Our purpose is not in this world but in God. If we remain in God, remain in His love, then we know that all things will be for our good as following and proclaiming the gospel of Christ is our purpose.* That is the key to understanding God's purpose for your life. God not only created us with a purpose, but He also numbered our days. He will take us home when our purpose has been fulfilled.

If you're like many of us, you'd love for God to spell out, in detail, His plan for our lives. We want to know what kind of job we're going to have, who we're going to marry if we're going to have children, and how many, and all the details we'd like and need to feel secure and confident that we're "in God's plan" for our lives. But God doesn't do that. He wants us to trust Him, to believe in Him, and to develop our faith in Him. *"And without faith, it is impossible to please God"* Hebrews 11:6

God created you (and every person on planet Earth) with the six basic categories listed here and elsewhere throughout this book:

- Emotional
- Physical
- Spiritual
- Social
- Psychological

SOARING FOR THE KINGDOM

- Purpose

First, God wants us to pursue our purpose — which is His purpose. He wants us to grow spiritually, socially, physically, and within our family and career. We can't grow if we don't set goals in each of those areas. God created you as a spiritual being. He wants you to love Him with your whole heart, soul, and mind (Matthew 22: 3). You can't do that if your goals aren't aligned with your spiritual conviction and God's laws. If you pursue your own goals and not God's purpose for you, expect to have problems in all areas of your life — physical, emotional, social, psychological, and spiritual.

It's not just sin that can derail you. God created us to seek fellowship and connection with other believers. That's the social aspect of our life. Even if you're spending 99 percent of your time in the Word, if you're not fellowshipping and interacting with others, you'll become out of balance and experience that imbalance in all those same areas — physical, emotional, social, and so on. When I talk about balance, I mean balance in all areas of our lives. If that feels like you're on a unicycle on top of a giant rubber ball balancing six spinning plates, I understand. It feels unmanageable. How can we ever manage to balance all those things? The good news is God helps us. He never intended for us to do it all by ourselves and then present our best efforts for His approval.

God is with us every step of the way — like a parent teaching and working with their child to help them grow and prosper.

Aspect Number Six — Seek a Purpose Balance

ACTION ITEMS

- **Determine what your purpose in life is at this stage.** Our purpose changes throughout our life. As children, we aim to obey our parents, learn about God, go to school, grow, and learn. As teens, our purpose changes as we consider our future career, whether we want a spouse and family or pursue a mission. Finding a balance for our purpose that changes as we age can sometimes be challenging. Remember, your purpose changes as you age, so think about where you are now, where you want to go, and what God's will is for you as you move forward.

- **Define your purpose.** For many of us, career, marriage, children, and family are our purpose once we've committed ourselves to seeking God and fulfilling His desire for our lives. Knowing where we are going helps us keep our eyes on the prize, so to speak, when we are tempted by unexpected opportunities. If, for instance, your purpose and goal are to attend college, then buying a new car instead of driving the one you have may derail your college goals. When we know what we want, and our purpose is clearly defined, we turn to that guiding light or goal before making decisions. For instance, if your child is saving to buy a bicycle or some other item and a chance to go on a trip to an amusement park arises that would seriously deplete their savings, you would have a talk with them about their choice and why they should focus on the goal versus the short-term fun of the park. Maybe they want the bike to get a paper route, have more mobility, or ride with their friends. Is it really worth putting off that goal for another month to three months to have one day of fun at an amusement park? What other options can they come up with? The same is true for us as adults. A long-term goal or short-term enjoyment?

SOARING FOR THE KINGDOM

- **List the top 10 reasons for your purpose.** This exercise is to help you strengthen and clarify the reason(s) for your purpose and make it easier to stay committed to it when times get hard. God will often test us to show us if our commitment is strong or in the right place, to begin with. Know why you do what you do or want to do. When we are confident about our goals, purpose, and commitments, it's easier to get through the tough times when we might doubt ourselves.

Chapter 12

SOARing High for the Kingdom

You did it! You've learned about and have begun to develop the skills and tools that will literally last you for an eternity in God's Kingdom. After going through this book, you should now know how to apply the four foundational aspects of *Soaring for the Kingdom*.

You should also now have a timeless set of tools you can always grab when you find yourself deflated, depressed, or demoralized. Just as a hammer and screwdriver are timeless tools for anyone to have, this book will be your timeless tool for learning how best to create a life for God. I hope you see the important benefit of making this book a tool for everyday use — either as a reference or as part of your daily quiet time. One way to do that is to spend a month reviewing and incorporating each chapter into your life. To this end, as I mentioned earlier, I have also created a journal to help you (available both on Amazon and on my website at www.kingdomecounter19.com.

So what can you expect now? If you continue to study and apply God's Word and develop The Six Skills to your life. Soaring in the Kingdom will be your life— leading the life God intended for you. But remember, SOARing is not without challenges and difficulties.

SOARING FOR THE KINGDOM

God didn't promise us a life of ease and prosperity here on Earth. If He had and had delivered that, everyone would accept Christ and follow Him. God did promise us many things, more than 3,000 things, actually! Here are some of my favorites:

- **God promises to strengthen us during hard times.** This is such a hard promise to claim because it often makes no sense. When things look like they couldn't get any darker or harder, suddenly, they do. A loved one dies, another is harmed in an accident or an attack through no fault of their own; our lives begin to crumble. Suddenly it's hard to believe God would not only allow these horrific things to happen but then strengthen us through the events and give us the grace and courage we need to accept His will and continue in our faith.

- **God promises to give us rest.** *"Then Jesus said, 'Come to me, all of you who are weary and carry heavy burdens, and I will give you rest. Take my yoke upon you. Let me teach* you *because I am humble and gentle at heart, and you will find rest for your souls. For my yoke is easy to bear, and the burden I give you is light,'"* (Matthew 11:28-30). There are so many times during the writing of this book I just wanted to lie down and sleep until everything was done and over. I was so tired. I had many, many challenges in my personal and work life to sort out as I wrote. Through it all, my soul did rest. I was deeply troubled, sleep-deprived, and challenged at every level, yet when I sought God, He did give me the rest I needed to continue.

- **God promises to take care of all our needs, emotional, spiritual, and yes, physical.** *"And this same God who takes care of me will supply all your needs from His glorious riches, which have been given to us in Christ Jesus,"* (Philippians 4:19). That promise doesn't mean God's going to send you a new home, a new car, a fat bank

146

SOARing High for the Kingdom

account, and a handsome or beautiful spouse. Although, He might. Our needs are the things we must have to survive. Ask a five or 10-year-old child what they "need," and their answers will be far different from what we, as their parents, know they truly need. God is our Heavenly Father, our parent; He sees what we need and what we want, and He acts accordingly, just as any good parent would.

- **God promises to answer our prayers**. "*Ask, and it will be given to you; seek, and you will find; knock, and it will be opened to you,*" (Matthew 7:7). His answers won't always be "yes," but He will give us an answer. Sometimes the answer is "yes," and sometimes, it's "no," and sometimes, it's "wait." No matter what the answer, it's for our best. God may also answer our prayers in ways we never expected and could never conceive of ourselves. I promise you that God's answers always exceed our wildest imagination. Trust Him.

- **God promises to work everything out for your good.** "*And we know that God causes everything to work together for the good of those who love God and are called according to his purpose for them,*" (Romans 8:28). I have had so many things happen to me that I believed were dead ends, destruction, and the loss of all I valued in life. I have seen my children harmed and my extended family die and struggle. From where I stood, I could see nothing good in anything that happened. And even today, I struggle to see the good where there appears to be only evil. I've cried out, as have you, "Why God?!" Whatever happens to us happens for God's reason, God's glory, and God's purposes. He did not promise us we'd always understand what happens to us, only that He has His reasons for whatever it is.

- **God promises to be with you no matter what.** "*I will not fail you or abandon you. This is my command — be strong and courageous! Do not be afraid or discouraged. For* the Lord *your God is with you wherever you go"* (Joshua 1:5, 9). Sometimes, God walks in front of us. Sometimes, He walks behind us or beside us, and sometimes, He carries us. But no matter what, He is always with us, whether we feel or sense His presence or not.

- **God promises that nothing can separate you from Him.** *"For I am sure that neither death nor life, nor angels nor rulers, nor things present nor things to come, nor powers, nor height nor depth, nor anything else in all creation, will be able to separate us from the love of God in Christ Jesus our Lord,"* (Romans 8:38-39). As an earthly, human parent, I cannot be always with my children to protect, advise, and look over them. But God can. And He does. He is the creator, Lord, and King and has the final say over everything that happens in the Universe. Nothing is greater, more powerful, more clever, or more loving than God. And He has promised us nothing can separate us from Him. The only thing that can come between us and God is unrepentant sin. But He has provided a way to eliminate that — Jesus Christ — if we just ask Him.

- **God promises to strengthen you.** *"For this* reason, *I bow my knees before the Father, from whom every family in heaven and on earth is named, that according to the riches of his glory he may grant you to be strengthened with power through his Spirit in your inner being,"* (Ephesians 3:14-16). What do we need most in this life? I believe it's God's strength. With His strength, we can do anything, and anything is possible. Even in the worst of times, God is there, providing us with the strength we need to keep going.

- **God promises to protect you from spiritual as well as physical attacks.** *"This I declare about the LORD: He alone is my refuge, my place of safety; he is my God, and I trust him"* (Psalm 91:2). We don't always know why bad things happen to good or innocent people if He is

SOARing High for the Kingdom

protecting us, but we do have to trust He has a plan. What He sees as protection isn't always what we see. He has a plan, and while we can't always see it, we can trust it. He is God, and He has promised to protect us, and He is.

- **God promises freedom from sin.** This is not freedom from temptation or the act of sinning itself. It's the freedom from the consequences (spiritual death) of sin.
- **God promises us eternal life.** *"For God so loved the world, that he gave his only Son, that whoever believes in him should not perish but have eternal life"* (John 3:16). Our time here on Earth is the blink of an eye in terms of eternity. Of all the things that God promises us, this is my favorite — the promise of eternity with God, our Father, Creator, and King. Is there anything better than the promise of eternal life in Heaven, with no sin, no tears, and no pain?

Another Bible study that will strengthen and grow your faith is to study God's promises to us as believers. Write down, learn about, and then claim those promises and track how He answers them. You'll be amazed and humbled by how generous, loving, and tender God is with us.

EMPOWERED

Throughout this book are the promises God has for us when we love, obey, and follow Him. Once you pursue God with all your heart, mind, soul, and strength and create these foundations with His help, you will have a feeling of being stronger after reading this material simply because you're drawing closer to God. My intention is to help you feel more confident as you do. Once you have a clearer idea of what to do and you begin spending time in the Word and getting to know God better, you will have feelings of being supported. Hopefully, you related to the material and information in the book and realize that you now have the *tools* to move forward in all aspects of your life. You have the power to SOAR for the Kingdom. All you need to do now is practice these methods, use the tools, and become proficient with them.

DETERMINED

Once you have developed a spirit of empowerment from being in the Word and getting to know God, you'll begin growing in your commitment to walking with God. As that happens, you should find yourself growing with a determined spirit to now serve others as well. But you are also determined because of the direction I have provided in this book — to not "over-spiritualize" your life. God has given us practical, everyday gifts that we can use on this earth. Remember the focus is *for the Kingdom*.

Additionally, we can often waiver to complete something. However, we need to make sure we finish what we commit to finish regardless of our feelings. Our word should be our bond. Emotions change minute by minute. Determine to stick with this process no matter how unmotivated or depressed you may become. Feelings are not facts. Only God's Word is 100 percent fact. Believe it, trust it, lean on it.

CHALLENGED

The attacks, both spiritual and physical, that we experience are part of our everyday lives. If we "over-spiritualize" we will not be able to function. The Bible, along with prayer and obedience to the Word, are the amazing tools that focus on giving us direction for our everyday lives.

These six aspects are so important to our growth as Christians. These aspects form the core of this book and will help you build your spiritual muscles in your everyday life. The more you build your spiritual muscles, the more resilient you will be. The more you can

SOARing High for the Kingdom

persevere, the more your faith will grow. Everything you commit to Christ — the more you do *through* Christ, the more you will be able to carry out what you need to do on Earth. As the Bible says, "Well done, thou good and faithful servant."

Everything here is about your motives here on Earth. The *how* is the quality you show in the work you do here on Earth. In other words, *how you go about your work matters.* There is no labor in Heaven. The labor part of life ends here on Earth. You don't want to get so spiritually minded you lose your Earthly abilities. You need to share in a way people can relate to. The goal in this book was to help you soar like an eagle. When a storm arises, the eagle flies *directly* into the heart of the storm. They are the only birds known to do so.

Eagles fly into the chaos of a storm, using the storm's current (chaos) and pressure **to rise higher and soar quickly.** The pressure of the storm (chaos) is used to help them glide without using their energy as their wings' unique design allows them to lock in a fixed position amid the violent storm winds. I marveled at this when I read about it. Troubled times are what strengthens our faith. It's when everything is going wrong that we turn to God.

When it rains, most birds head for shelter; the eagle is the only bird that, to avoid the rain, actually soars into it, and through it to the eye of the storm.

The reason the eagle does this is that because in the eye of the storm, the sun is shining, the birds are chirping — it is quiet. The eagle knows that there is another bad part of the storm on the other side. But once in the middle, they know they are closer to the end. They don't fear storms, they embrace them, knowing they'll soar more quickly.

The eagle teaches you to *push through dark days, to push through anxiety, to push through frustration, to soar on the pressure of the storm.*

SOARING FOR THE KINGDOM

Do not give up on your dreams. Do not give up on yourself or your life. When most people face challenges, they start doubting themselves. They lose confidence. These attacks are both mental and spiritual. Most come from the forces of darkness, others from our own sinful nature and doubts. Wherever they originate, they are coming,intending to cause people to shrink back, doubt, and quit or give up. This is about knowing that these times of doubt, low self-esteem, and low self-confidence, will pass. The *enemy* knows this. But with Jesus *all things are possible.*

ENCOURAGED

Encouragement is all about giving us help. Christ is the God of Hope. Hope means an expectation of something better happening in our future, even if things seem bleak and hopeless right now. No matter what happens here on Earth, our number-one expectation with hope is that we will spend eternity with God. When you start to feel deflated and need that boost of hope, turn to the Word. Nothing will encourage or uplift you more than reading about David's struggles, and God's answers to his prayers for encouragement and support.

Being in God's Word and reading about how God encouraged His leaders is like attending a pep rally. Encouragement from the Word, other believers, and your prayer or gratitude journal create the energy and a sense of awareness that you can win and will win and have already won because God is on your side. It's crucial to "gather together" for the sole purpose of encouraging one another and supporting those who are struggling, as well as getting support for our struggles. God never intended for any of us to go through life alone. The purpose of encouraging one another is primarily to stimulate the resolve, most specifically of the players. In life here on Earth, we are the players — the Kingdom players.

CONVICTION

Conviction holds negative connotations for most of us. It feels like a criticism, a thing with only negative connotations. This word likely seems out of place. However, we are talking here about a spiritual conviction, not human criticism. We often have opinions that are not always in alignment with God's Word. I have paid particular attention to the situations that arise in our daily lives. These are situations that have many of us feeling conflicted. By sharing a wide variety of examples of what others, including myself, have gone through, I hope to help you get back into alignment on your walk with God.

Perhaps the most meaningful advice I can offer is to prioritize your results, not your actions. Set a goal, then work backward to see what you need to do to achieve that goal.

CUT THE CLUTTER

As you work through these steps and pursue Kingdom life, begin to *cut the clutter* in your life. I used to work with Nestle USA. Every three months, we devoted an entire day to cutting and clearing out the clutter in our respective departments. After a decluttering day, we all felt much better, more energized, and more positive. So here, you have to *cut your clutter* — the spiritual clutter, your heart clutter, etc., and yes, if necessary, the physical clutter in your home, office, car, and environment. Studies show that we not only feel better, lose weight, think more clearly, and are more productive when we declutter but also sleep better and have better relationships.

IMMEDIATE RESULTS

The journey of a thousand miles begins with one step. Do not rush your journey or try to learn and apply all these things simultaneously.

SOARING FOR THE KINGDOM

Begin with one step, one chapter. The Holy Spirit will impress upon, or bring to mind, the things you should focus on first. Spend consistent, small doses of time with God through his Word, in prayer, in workshops, or in study. You don't have to spend hours doing this. In time, you will crave God's presence, so many hours will fly by like minutes, but to start, get your special place together in five minutes. Don't take on these tasks for an hour. Five minutes is enough to start. The important thing is to start.

Where do you start? Start by getting rid of *toxic relationships*. Toxic relationships are any relationships that deter or detract from your pursuit of God or that lead you into sin. They may feel wonderful and supportive, and positive, but if they aren't getting you closer to soaring for the Kingdom, or they're violating God's laws or Word, Eliminate all that is toxic. Toxicity left in the body for too long will lead to harmful, life-threatening problems. For you to soar in a whole and healthy manner, all toxins will have to be eliminated from the heart, mind, and spirit.

That friend who loves to get together and socialize and gossip, drink, or party, and who makes you laugh, but at the expense of others, may need to go, or they may need to be confronted. Just because someone says they're a Christian and goes to church, they may not be a true believer. Many people attend church like it's another social media opportunity. They want to meet people, network and socialize. Their reasons for being there have little to do with walking with Christ, believing in God, and going to Heaven.

You may enjoy these people and their friendship. You may not see them as toxic, even if they gossip. After all, you say, "Everybody gossips, and besides, they're good people. They help out at church, do good things, and mean well."

However, God abhors gossips and busybodies. The Hebrew word translated as "gossip" in the Old Testament is defined as "one who reveals secrets, one who goes about as a talebearer or scandal-monger."

A gossiper is a person who has privileged information about people and proceeds to reveal that information to those who have no business knowing it.[1] Ah! Harder than you thought? When God says "toxic," He means anyone and anything that comes between you and your relationship with Him. That person may be a non-believer but a "good person" who helps others but who practices a different religion or belief — like New Age practices.

I guarantee you that the minute you follow God and spend time in the Word, Satan will use those toxic relationships to keep you from doing so. The devil doesn't come at us, roaring with hellfire and brimstone. He comes to us with charm and lies that sound plausible and harmless. Remember the Garden of Eden? The serpent approached Eve with a simple question to get her to doubt God.

"Did God really say, 'You must not eat from any tree in the garden?' The woman said to the serpent, 'We may eat fruit from the trees in the garden,' but God did say, 'You must not eat fruit from the tree that is in the middle of the garden, and you must not touch it, or you will die.' 'You will not certainly die,' the serpent said to the woman. 'For God knows that when you eat from it your eyes will be opened, and you will be like God, knowing good and evil'" (Genesis 3:1-5).

Satan rarely just throws an obvious temptation at us. He starts with small thoughts and temptations. He casts doubts upon God and what His word says. "Did God really say ... " he asked Eve? He began to implant a seed of doubt in her regarding not only God's commandment regarding the fruit from the tree but God's intent for her. What started as a seemingly innocent conversation turned into a sin that impacted all of humanity.

If you want to see immediate results, you must get rid of toxic relationships. Many of us think, "If I had been Eve, I would've said

SOARING FOR THE KINGDOM

'no' to the serpent." Yet, we cannot say no to the littlest of temptations Satan presents to us each day!

I cannot understand the logic of people continuing toxic relationships. You cannot get off the ground, let alone soar, when surrounded by these relationships. The Bible says this is *weight* and *sin*. You will not be able to soar as long as you're around those who hold you back. I know that those relationships you most need to give up — that non-believing boyfriend or girlfriend, or that best friend who happens to be "spiritual" but not Christian, may be some great friends. But they're toxic because they stand between you and God.

Toxic relationships can be subtle. Satan didn't try to tempt Eve when Adam was with her. He got her alone, so no one was there to stop her or interrupt or challenge what he was saying. Notice the serpent didn't introduce himself. Their conversation was one of two beings who knew each other. Maybe Eve had talked to him before or seen him from afar. We don't know. We do know she trusted him and was comfortable talking to him alone. That's how the tempter works, subtly. He won't tell you, "Don't have a quiet time this morning. Sleep in another half an hour instead. You know you're tired and work hard and deserve it. You can catch up tomorrow." And then tomorrow, he says the same thing until your quiet time with God has been effectively derailed. Eve's first mistake was giving him a foothold in her life. Satan doesn't need much of a foothold to enter our lives. This is why we are called never to give place to the devil.

> " ... be renewed in the spirit of your mind; And that ye put on the new man, which after God is created in righteousness and true holiness. Wherefore, putting away lying, speak every man truth with his neighbor: for we are members of one another. Be ye angry, and sin not: let not the sun go down upon your wrath: Neither gives place to the devil"

> — Ephesians 4:23

Don't think you can hold your own with Satan. Even Michael, the Archangel of God, told Satan, "The Lord rebuke you," when he encountered him. That means no discussion, no curious or wondering thoughts about his opinions is allowed. There is to be no giving him a chance to gain a foothold in our lives. Satan will use that foothold, no matter how small, to weasel his way into our lives. All he had to do with Eve is suggest that maybe God didn't say something she knew He did.

The same happens with us. That "spiritual" friend may agree to read this book if you read one of hers. That seems innocent enough, but chances are you'll read her book, and she won't read this one. The conversation about "God and spiritual things" will lead to discussing the New Age or other non-biblical things. You'll probably go along with her, hoping to win her over for Christ. But Satan will do to you what he did to Eve. He'll twist God's words and meanings until you doubt the Word. Don't give Satan that chance. Find other Bible-believing Christians to hang with. If you don't know any, ask God to bring them into your life. He will.

Next, change your vocabulary. The Bible says the power of life and death is on the tongue. We are never given the ability to speak things into existence, but our words can and do influence and impact others. Many prosperity preachers like to twist God's words so that we believe all we have to do is "name it and claim it" or use mystical power to manifest things, people, or money into our lives. That's not biblical. It sounds like the truth, but Satan has again taken and twisted God's Word to convince us to sin. God is the only creator and thus, only He can create things with His Word.

Our words can create good and bad actions based on our speech. As GotQuestions.org explains so well:

"A judge or jury, by simply saying a word, can cause a person to be killed or to live. Words often save lives: a doctor advises surgery, a weatherman issues a tornado warning, or a counselor gives hope to a suicidal person. Conversely, words can also kill. Murders are often initiated because of arguments or verbalized hatred. In the sense of causing action, then, the tongue does indeed have the power of life and death."[2]

Our words can destroy or encourage things that exist or crush another's soul. But God Himself is the only being who can create anything. He calls upon us to be careful of our speech lest we harm another or ourselves. *"Wise speech is rarer and more valuable than gold and rubies,"* (Proverbs 20:15).

Our tongues are powerful, but not because we are creating anything. Our tongue reveals what is in our heart — thus, our words have an eternal consequence. Jesus said, *"The good man brings good things out of the good stored up in him, and the evil man brings evil things out of the evil stored up in him,"* (Matthew 12:35).

Guard your tongue and watch what comes from it. It's the best indication of what lies in your heart.

Finally, rest and trust God with the process of your life and believe God's outcome for you can only be good, no matter how challenging or bad things seem to be now. Job's losses may have all occurred in one day, but the fallout lasted much longer. According to Job 2:13, Job's friends sat with him for seven days and seven nights without speaking when he was covered with boils. We don't know how long he suffered before they came or how long he suffered after they left.

Job doesn't mention years, only days and months when he speaks of his afflictions. From that, we can surmise he suffered for at least months, but probably less than a year. This was a man who had done nothing wrong, but whom Satan merely wanted to test. Yet, in the end, after all his losses and suffering, God returned all his property and the things he lost.

Trust God no matter what storms are raging. My favorite illustration of this concept is the image of a hurricane or tornado ripping up

SOARing High for the Kingdom

homes and land, and lives. Yet, above the storm and the chaos, the heavens are calm and clear. The confusion of the storm obscures that truth. We look up, and like Dorothy in *The Wizard of Oz*, all we see are broken pieces of our life swirling around us. But above the storm, God reigns supreme and is in control of everything — Satan, our enemies, our circumstances, and our confusion. Trust that God is there, and He is the one in control.

> *"But the Lord is with me like a mighty warrior; so my persecutors will stumble and not prevail. They will fail and be thoroughly disgraced; their dishonor will never be forgotten."*
>
> *— Jeremiah 20:11*

God made sure that his people knew to rest and to trust Him to meet their needs. How many of us who, when going through tumultuous times, know without a doubt, that God will bring us through? You will as you move forward, pray, immerse yourself in the Word of God, have faith, and trust Him. For without faith, it is impossible to please Him. If you follow the foundations and aspects in this book, you will develop the faith that pleases God, and you will find yourself soaring for the Kingdom!

ACTION ITEMS

- **List the top five takeaways from reading this book.** What stood out to you most? What did your spirit say? Did God speak to you about any specific topic? What was it?
- **Take time to think about, pray about, and decide where you want to go from here. Journal this process and your thoughts and feelings about it.** Some people will decide they don't have enough time, energy, or desire to commit to pursuing a balanced life right now. It is a lot of work, and it is a huge commitment. Better to commit to one thing or area of your life and succeed than to jump into a whole-person makeover that fails. Many of those who followed Christ later turned and left Him when they realized He wasn't going to be the ruling Messiah they thought He was. Many who realize God is not Santa Claus or an ATM who will make them rich and grant their heart's desire (a prosperity gospel promise) decide to forsake Christ as well.
- **Consider fasting for one, two, or three days while you seek God's will and desires for you after reading this book.** Fasting is a big step, but nothing I've done or found brings us closer to God than a 24-, 48-, or 72-hour fast.

Before You Go

It has been a great pleasure to have you walk with me through this book. I pray that it has met your needs, answered any questions you may have, and perhaps most importantly, touched your heart. I know that sharing all that I possibly can with you has truly touched my heart. If this book has helped you in any way, please reach out to me here at: **delsachristian@kingdomencounter19.com.** I look forward to helping you and soaring with you. If you enjoyed this book, then you can make a difference. How? Reviews are powerful. Honest book reviews help others locate books that can make a significant difference in your life. I would be very grateful if you could spend just five minutes leaving a review (it can be as short as you like). Just look up this book on Amazon along with my name, and thank you so much, in advance, for taking the time to write a review.

Acknowledgments

I thank all who contributed to the completion of Soaring for the Kingdom in one way or another. First, I thank God for his guidance, protection, and ability to do the work.

I want to thank my husband, Lee, for his unwavering support and encouragement. My son Percy always challenges me to go higher and reach more people, and my daughter London pushes me to do all God has for me to do. I also want to thank two extraordinary ladies in my life first, my mom, who molded me to soar to only greatness at a young age, and my mom in love, who has been a source of support for over thirty years, but I especially thank her for both verbal and her monetary investment with this project.

I greatly thank my dearest friend from childhood, Nikita, who always makes her support visible. Thank you to my armor-bearer Sharonda who constantly pushes me to reach for never-ending creative possibilities.

I am also profoundly grateful for my editors, Melissa G Wilson and Becky Blanton. I greatly appreciated their help, research, and belief in this book and me.

I greatly thank and appreciate ALL who spoke positive words into my heart. Your word seeds of love and unwavering support fell on good ground and lodged in my heart.

Lastly, I thank my father, who is no longer with me on earth. I am grateful for my years with him being an example to never-give-up, endure through all things, and have a deep work ethic. I know he would be in my corner as a proud father supporting his "baby girl," the author.

About the Author

Delsa D. Christian is an ordained prophet, minister, prayer warrior, blogger, author, conference speaker, and business owner. She seeks to inspire and motivate others by fostering the belief that they can do all things through Christ.

Delsa Christian is the Executive Pastor of City of Hope Family Worship Center, Women's Ministry Director, facilitating women's Bible Studies, workshops, and developing bible studies for ladies. Prophetess Christian is the founder of "Treasures from the Heart" and Kingdom Encounter Ministries, launched on September 27, 2019, and author of Prayer Journal, Your 90-Day Prayer Journal-For Cleansing, Refreshing, and Receiving, and Soaring for the Kingdom.

Delsa Christian is currently working on her Master's degree in Women's Leadership with plans to complete her Doctorate of Ministry in Apolostlic Leadership. She desires to help women lead, arise, shine in this new era for Apostolic women, and have spiritual balance, emotional health, and self-care. Prophetess Christian's heart desires that the Lord will use her to help women love themselves and see themselves as Christ sees them- "Created in His Image" and help them become whole and healed vessels equipped to lead for the Master's use.

With God the Father, she is on a mission to eradicate the phrases "I cannot" and "I do not know how" from daily use because she believes that we can change our vision and world by changing our vocabularies. She believes this passion is in alignment with the Word of God. She believes that when the Spirit of God and the Word of God come together and flow through His people, things are created, altered, and destroyed.

The Earth was without form and void, and darkness was on the face of the deep. And the Spirit of God was hovering (MOVING) over the face of the waters. Then God said... Genesis 1:2-3 (a) NKJ

For over 20 years, she has held leadership and management positions in various Fortune 500 companies and organizations. Her mission is to partner with individuals, companies, and nonprofit organizations to help them grow and learn. She wants more people to live Kingdom lives of impact and significance.

"Believing in yourself and inspiring others to do the same are the keys to accomplishment, achievement, and a purpose-filled life." – Delsa Christian

Delsa is the founder of Kingdom Encounter Ministries, which offers speaking, training, and coaching in discipleship, growth, development, communication, and leadership. She is also the C.E.O. founder of Heaven's Press Publishing, a publishing firm that focuses on faith-based books. Delsa is always excited about a future of unlimited possibilities, not focusing on the past or getting stuck in the present.

Prophetess Delsa Christian is excited about her "chosen" position in the Kingdom of God. She enjoys serving God's people, His Word in the spirit of Love and Compassion, and spending intimate time with her Lord (Master) and Raboni (Teacher). She feels it's a blessing to be a "chosen" vessel for the Master's use.

Her motto is: Jesus is my EVERYTHING and "I am In His Hands!-" He carried me through my past, He's carrying me in my present, and therefore, I know my future is already HANDLED!

Notes

1. Spiritual Nourishment

1. ttps://www.cgg.org/index.cfm/library/verses/id/1614/nourishment-spiritual-verses.htm

2. Organize Your Life

1. (Indiana University and Keith) Indiana University, and Nicole Keith. "Tidier homes, fitter bodies?" *https://newsinfo.iu.edu*, Indiana University, 2013, https://www.psychologytoday.com/us/blog/the-truisms-wellness/201607/the-powerful-psychology-behind-cleanliness. Accessed 23 August 2021.
2. Indiana University, and Nicole Keith. "Tidier homes, fitter bodies?" *https://newsinfo.iu.edu*, Indiana University, 2013, https://www.psychologytoday.com/us/blog/the-truisms-wellness/201607/the-powerful-psychology-behind-cleanliness. Accessed 23 August 2021.
3. Scientific American, and Christine Gorman. "Medicine Nobel Recognizes "Self-Eating" Cells." *ScientificAmerican.com*, Scientific American, 3 October 2016, https://www.scientificamerican.com/article/medicine-nobel-recognizes-self-eating-cell-research/. Accessed 23 August 2021.
4. Healthline. "Autophagy: What You Need to Know." *Healthline.com*, Healthline, 23 August 2018, https://www.healthline.com/health/autophagy#diet. Accessed 23 August 2021.
5. (1 Corinthians 5 and in 1 Corinthians 2:9 and 7:12)
6. Forbes, and Andria Cheng. "Amazon Ships 2.5 Billion Packages a Year, With Billions More Coming, In a Major Threat To UPS And FedEx." *Forbes.com*, Forbes, 12 December 2019, https://www.forbes.com/sites/andriacheng/2019/12/12/how-serious-is-amazons-threat-to-ups-fedex-study-finds-it-could-soon-beat-them-in-us-package-delivery-volume/?sh=4d0774ab68f4. Accessed 23 August 23 2021.
7. Wall Street Journal, and Jennifer Levitz. "Delivery Drivers to Pick up Pace by Surrendering Keys." *WSJ.com*, Wall Street Journal, 16 September 2011, https://www.wsj.com/articles/SB10001424053111904060604576572891040895366. Accessed 23 August 2021.
8. Westby, Kenneth. *The Amazing Seven Day Cycle*. 1 ed., vol. 1, Kenneth Westby, 1990, http://docshare01.docshare.tips/files/2972/29728901.pdf. Accessed 24 August 2021.
9. Westby, Kenneth. *The Amazing Seven Day Cycle*. 1 ed., vol. 1, Kenneth Westby, 1990, http://docshare01.docshare.tips/files/2972/29728901.pdf. Accessed 24

Notes

August 2021.

10. Biggs, Carolyn. "Study Reveals the Most Common Items that Go Missing at Home." *Apartment Therapy*, Apartment Therapy, 29 June 2017, Study Reveals the Most Common Items that Go Missing at Home. Accessed 23 September 2021.

3. Accountable To God And Man

1. Leadership Ministries. "What About Biblical Accountability?" *Leadmin.org*, Leadership Ministries, 6 August 2019, https://leadmin.org/articles/what-about-biblical-accountability. Accessed 23 August 2021.
2. Leadership Ministries. "What About Biblical Accountability?" *Leadmin.org*, Leadership Ministries, 6 August 2019, https://leadmin.org/articles/what-about-biblical-accountability. Accessed 23 August 2021.

4. Release Yourself from all Encumbrances

1. Blue Letter Bible. "The Gospel of Luke." *BlueLetterBible.org*, https://www.blueletterbible.org/study/intros/luke.cfm. Accessed 30 August 2021.

5. The Six Aspects of Living: An Overview of the Basic Structure of All Human Beings

1. Hougaard, R., et al. *One Second Ahead*. New York, Palgrave McMillian. *Emotional Balance*, https://doi.org/10.1057/9781137551924_16. Accessed 30 August 2021.

6. Aspect Number One: Seek an Emotional Balance

1. Hougaard, R., et al. *One Second Ahead*. New York, Palgrave McMillian. *Emotional Balance*, https://doi.org/10.1057/9781137551924_16. Accessed 30 August 2021.

11. Aspect Number Six – Seek a Purpose Balance

1. "Christianity - What compelled the fishermen to immediately follow Jesus." *Christianity*, https://christianity.stackexchange.com/questions/40379/what-

Notes

compelled-the-fishermen-to-immediately-follow-jesus. Accessed 6 September 2021.

12. SOARing High for the Kingdom

1. GotQuestions. *What does the Bible say about gossip?* GotQuestions. *GotQuestions.org*, https://www.gotquestions.org/gossip-Bible.html. Accessed 24 September 2021.
2. GotQuestions.org. "Is it true that life and death are in the power of the tongue?" *GotQuestions.org*, Got Questions, https://www.gotquestions.org/power-of-the-tongue.html. Accessed 25 September 2021.

Made in the USA
Middletown, DE
17 November 2022

15066848R00102